Iowa

Assessments
Success Strategies
Level 13 Grade 7

DEAR FUTURE EXAM SUCCESS STORY

First of all, **THANK YOU** for purchasing Mometrix study materials!

Second, congratulations! You are one of the few determined test-takers who are committed to doing whatever it takes to excel on your exam. **You have come to the right place.** We developed these study materials with one goal in mind: to deliver you the information you need in a format that's concise and easy to use.

In addition to optimizing your guide for the content of the test, we've outlined our recommended steps for breaking down the preparation process into small, attainable goals so you can make sure you stay on track.

We've also analyzed the entire test-taking process, identifying the most common pitfalls and showing how you can overcome them and be ready for any curveball the test throws you.

Standardized testing is one of the biggest obstacles on your road to success, which only increases the importance of doing well in the high-pressure, high-stakes environment of test day. Your results on this test could have a significant impact on your future, and this guide provides the information and practical advice to help you achieve your full potential on test day.

Your success is our success

We would love to hear from you! If you would like to share the story of your exam success or if you have any questions or comments in regard to our products, please contact us at **800-673-8175** or **support@mometrix.com**.

Thanks again for your business and we wish you continued success!

Sincerely,
The Mometrix Test Preparation Team

TABLE OF CONTENTS

Introduction

Thank you for purchasing this resource! You have made the choice to prepare yourself for a test that could have a huge impact on your future, and this guide is designed to help you be fully ready for test day. Obviously, it's important to have a solid understanding of the test material, but you also need to be prepared for the unique environment and stressors of the test, so that you can perform to the best of your abilities.

For this purpose, the first section that appears in this guide is the **Success Strategies**. We've devoted countless hours to meticulously researching what works and what doesn't, and we've boiled down our findings to the five most impactful steps you can take to improve your performance on the test. We start at the beginning with study planning and move through the preparation process, all the way to the testing strategies that will help you get the most out of what you know when you're finally sitting in front of the test.

We recommend that you start preparing for your test as far in advance as possible. However, if you've bought this guide as a last-minute study resource and only have a few days before your test, we recommend that you skip over the first two Success Strategies since they address a long-term study plan.

If you struggle with **test anxiety**, we strongly encourage you to check out our recommendations for how you can overcome it. Test anxiety is a formidable foe, but it can be beaten, and we want to make sure you have the tools you need to defeat it.

Strategy #1 – Plan Big, Study Small

There's a lot riding on your performance. If you want to ace this test, you're going to need to keep your skills sharp and the material fresh in your mind. You need a plan that lets you review everything you need to know while still fitting in your schedule. We'll break this strategy down into three categories.

Information Organization

Start with the information you already have: the official test outline. From this, you can make a complete list of all the concepts you need to cover before the test. Organize these concepts into groups that can be studied together, and create a list of any related vocabulary you need to learn so you can brush up on any difficult terms. You'll want to keep this vocabulary list handy once you actually start studying since you may need to add to it along the way.

Time Management

Once you have your set of study concepts, decide how to spread them out over the time you have left before the test. Break your study plan into small, clear goals so you have a manageable task for each day and know exactly what you're doing. Then just focus on one small step at a time. When you manage your time this way, you don't need to spend hours at a time studying. Studying a small block of content for a short period each day helps you retain information better and avoid stressing over how much you have left to do. You can relax knowing that you have a plan to cover everything in time. In order for this strategy to be effective though, you have to start studying early and stick to your schedule. Avoid the exhaustion and futility that comes from last-minute cramming!

Study Environment

The environment you study in has a big impact on your learning. Studying in a coffee shop, while probably more enjoyable, is not likely to be as fruitful as studying in a quiet room. It's important to keep distractions to a minimum. You're only planning to study for a short block of time, so make the most of it. Don't pause to check your phone or get up to find a snack. It's also important to **avoid multitasking**. Research has consistently shown that multitasking will make your studying dramatically less effective. Your study area should also be comfortable and well-lit so you don't have the distraction of straining your eyes or sitting on an uncomfortable chair.

 The time of day you study is also important. You want to be rested and alert. Don't wait until just before bedtime. Study when you'll be most likely to comprehend and remember. Even better, if you know what time of day your test will be, set that time aside for study. That way your brain will be used to working on that subject at that specific time and you'll have a better chance of recalling information.

Finally, it can be helpful to team up with others who are studying for the same test. Your actual studying should be done in as isolated an environment as possible, but the work of organizing the information and setting up the study plan can be divided up. In between study sessions, you can discuss with your teammates the concepts that you're all studying and quiz each other on the details. Just be sure that your teammates are as serious about the test as you are. If you find that your study time is being replaced with social time, you might need to find a new team.

2

Strategy #2 – Make Your Studying Count

You're devoting a lot of time and effort to preparing for this test, so you want to be absolutely certain it will pay off. This means doing more than just reading the content and hoping you can remember it on test day. It's important to make every minute of study count. There are two main areas you can focus on to make your studying count.

Retention

It doesn't matter how much time you study if you can't remember the material. You need to make sure you are retaining the concepts. To check your retention of the information you're learning, try recalling it at later times with minimal prompting. Try carrying around flashcards and glance at one or two from time to time or ask a friend who's also studying for the test to quiz you.

To enhance your retention, look for ways to put the information into practice so that you can apply it rather than simply recalling it. If you're using the information in practical ways, it will be much easier to remember. Similarly, it helps to solidify a concept in your mind if you're not only reading it to yourself but also explaining it to someone else. Ask a friend to let you teach them about a concept you're a little shaky on (or speak aloud to an imaginary audience if necessary). As you try to summarize, define, give examples, and answer your friend's questions, you'll understand the concepts better and they will stay with you longer. Finally, step back for a big picture view and ask yourself how each piece of information fits with the whole subject. When you link the different concepts together and see them working together as a whole, it's easier to remember the individual components.

Finally, practice showing your work on any multi-step problems, even if you're just studying. Writing out each step you take to solve a problem will help solidify the process in your mind, and you'll be more likely to remember it during the test.

Modality

Modality simply refers to the means or method by which you study. Choosing a study modality that fits your own individual learning style is crucial. No two people learn best in exactly the same way, so it's important to know your strengths and use them to your advantage.

For example, if you learn best by visualization, focus on visualizing a concept in your mind and draw an image or a diagram. Try color-coding your notes, illustrating them, or creating symbols that will trigger your mind to recall a learned concept. If you learn best by hearing or discussing information, find a study partner who learns the same way or read aloud to yourself. Think about how to put the information in your own words. Imagine that you are giving a lecture on the topic and record yourself so you can listen to it later.

For any learning style, flashcards can be helpful. Organize the information so you can take advantage of spare moments to review. Underline key words or phrases. Use different colors for different categories. Mnemonic devices (such as creating a short list in which every item starts with the same letter) can also help with retention. Find what works best for you and use it to store the information in your mind most effectively and easily.

Strategy #3 – Practice the Right Way

Your success on test day depends not only on how many hours you put into preparing, but also on whether you prepared the right way. It's good to check along the way to see if your studying is paying off. One of the most effective ways to do this is by taking practice tests to evaluate your progress. Practice tests are useful because they show exactly where you need to improve. Every time you take a practice test, pay special attention to these three groups of questions:

- The questions you got wrong
- The questions you had to guess on, even if you guessed right
- The questions you found difficult or slow to work through

This will show you exactly what your weak areas are, and where you need to devote more study time. Ask yourself why each of these questions gave you trouble. Was it because you didn't understand the material? Was it because you didn't remember the vocabulary? Do you need more repetitions on this type of question to build speed and confidence? Dig into those questions and figure out how you can strengthen your weak areas as you go back to review the material.

 Additionally, many practice tests have a section explaining the answer choices. It can be tempting to read the explanation and think that you now have a good understanding of the concept. However, an explanation likely only covers part of the question's broader context. Even if the explanation makes perfect sense, **go back and investigate** every concept related to the question until you're positive you have a thorough understanding.

As you go along, keep in mind that the practice test is just that: practice. Memorizing these questions and answers will not be very helpful on the actual test because it is unlikely to have any of the same exact questions. If you only know the right answers to the sample questions, you won't be prepared for the real thing. **Study the concepts** until you understand them fully, and then you'll be able to answer any question that shows up on the test.

It's important to wait on the practice tests until you're ready. If you take a test on your first day of study, you may be overwhelmed by the amount of material covered and how much you need to learn. Work up to it gradually.

On test day, you'll need to be prepared for answering questions, managing your time, and using the test-taking strategies you've learned. It's a lot to balance, like a mental marathon that will have a big impact on your future. Like training for a marathon, you'll need to start slowly and work your way up. When test day arrives, you'll be ready.

Start with the strategies you've read in the first two Success Strategies—plan your course and study in the way that works best for you. If you have time, consider using multiple study resources to get different approaches to the same concepts. It can be helpful to see difficult concepts from more than one angle. Then find a good source for practice tests. Many times, the test website will suggest potential study resources or provide sample tests.

Practice Test Strategy

If you're able to find at least three practice tests, we recommend this strategy:

UNTIMED AND OPEN-BOOK PRACTICE

Take the first test with no time constraints and with your notes and study guide handy. Take your time and focus on applying the strategies you've learned.

TIMED AND OPEN-BOOK PRACTICE

Take the second practice test open-book as well, but set a timer and practice pacing yourself to finish in time.

TIMED AND CLOSED-BOOK PRACTICE

Take any other practice tests as if it were test day. Set a timer and put away your study materials. Sit at a table or desk in a quiet room, imagine yourself at the testing center, and answer questions as quickly and accurately as possible.

Keep repeating timed and closed-book tests on a regular basis until you run out of practice tests or it's time for the actual test. Your mind will be ready for the schedule and stress of test day, and you'll be able to focus on recalling the material you've learned.

Strategy #4 – Pace Yourself

Once you're fully prepared for the material on the test, your biggest challenge on test day will be managing your time. Just knowing that the clock is ticking can make you panic even if you have plenty of time left. Work on pacing yourself so you can build confidence against the time constraints of the exam. Pacing is a difficult skill to master, especially in a high-pressure environment, so **practice is vital**.

Set time expectations for your pace based on how much time is available. For example, if a section has 60 questions and the time limit is 30 minutes, you know you have to average 30 seconds or less per question in order to answer them all. Although 30 seconds is the hard limit, set 25 seconds per question as your goal, so you reserve extra time to spend on harder questions. When you budget extra time for the harder questions, you no longer have any reason to stress when those questions take longer to answer.

Don't let this time expectation distract you from working through the test at a calm, steady pace, but keep it in mind so you don't spend too much time on any one question. Recognize that taking extra time on one question you don't understand may keep you from answering two that you do understand later in the test. If your time limit for a question is up and you're still not sure of the answer, mark it and move on, and come back to it later if the time and the test format allow. If the testing format doesn't allow you to return to earlier questions, just make an educated guess; then put it out of your mind and move on.

On the easier questions, be careful not to rush. It may seem wise to hurry through them so you have more time for the challenging ones, but it's not worth missing one if you know the concept and just didn't take the time to read the question fully. Work efficiently but make sure you understand the question and have looked at all of the answer choices, since more than one may seem right at first.

Even if you're paying attention to the time, you may find yourself a little behind at some point. You should speed up to get back on track, but do so wisely. Don't panic; just take a few seconds less on each question until you're caught up. Don't guess without thinking, but do look through the answer choices and eliminate any you know are wrong. If you can get down to two choices, it is often worthwhile to guess from those. Once you've chosen an answer, move on and don't dwell on any that you skipped or had to hurry through. If a question was taking too long, chances are it was one of the harder ones, so you weren't as likely to get it right anyway.

On the other hand, if you find yourself getting ahead of schedule, it may be beneficial to slow down a little. The more quickly you work, the more likely you are to make a careless mistake that will affect your score. You've budgeted time for each question, so don't be afraid to spend that time. Practice an efficient but careful pace to get the most out of the time you have.

6

Test-Taking Strategies

This section contains a list of test-taking strategies that you may find helpful as you work through the test. By taking what you know and applying logical thought, you can maximize your chances of answering any question correctly!

It is very important to realize that every question is different and every person is different: no single strategy will work on every question, and no single strategy will work for every person. That's why we've included all of them here, so you can try them out and determine which ones work best for different types of questions and which ones work best for you.

Question Strategies

⊘ READ CAREFULLY

Read the question and the answer choices carefully. Don't miss the question because you misread the terms. You have plenty of time to read each question thoroughly and make sure you understand what is being asked. Yet a happy medium must be attained, so don't waste too much time. You must read carefully and efficiently.

⊘ CONTEXTUAL CLUES

Look for contextual clues. If the question includes a word you are not familiar with, look at the immediate context for some indication of what the word might mean. Contextual clues can often give you all the information you need to decipher the meaning of an unfamiliar word. Even if you can't determine the meaning, you may be able to narrow down the possibilities enough to make a solid guess at the answer to the question.

⊘ PREFIXES

If you're having trouble with a word in the question or answer choices, try dissecting it. Take advantage of every clue that the word might include. Prefixes can be a huge help. Usually, they allow you to determine a basic meaning. *Pre-* means before, *post-* means after, *pro-* is positive, *de-* is negative. From prefixes, you can get an idea of the general meaning of the word and try to put it into context.

⊘ HEDGE WORDS

Watch out for critical hedge words, such as *likely, may, can, sometimes, often, almost, mostly, usually, generally, rarely,* and *sometimes.* Question writers insert these hedge phrases to cover every possibility. Often an answer choice will be wrong simply because it leaves no room for exception. Be on guard for answer choices that have definitive words such as *exactly* and *always.*

⊘ SWITCHBACK WORDS

Stay alert for *switchbacks.* These are the words and phrases frequently used to alert you to shifts in thought. The most common switchback words are *but, although,* and *however.* Others include *nevertheless, on the other hand, even though, while, in spite of, despite,* and *regardless of.* Switchback words are important to catch because they can change the direction of the question or an answer choice.

⏱ FACE VALUE

When in doubt, use common sense. Accept the situation in the problem at face value. Don't read too much into it. These problems will not require you to make wild assumptions. If you have to go beyond creativity and warp time or space in order to have an answer choice fit the question, then you should move on and consider the other answer choices. These are normal problems rooted in reality. The applicable relationship or explanation may not be readily apparent, but it is there for you to figure out. Use your common sense to interpret anything that isn't clear.

Answer Choice Strategies

⏱ ANSWER SELECTION

The most thorough way to pick an answer choice is to identify and eliminate wrong answers until only one is left, then confirm it is the correct answer. Sometimes an answer choice may immediately seem right, but be careful. The test writers will usually put more than one reasonable answer choice on each question, so take a second to read all of them and make sure that the other choices are not equally obvious. As long as you have time left, it is better to read every answer choice than to pick the first one that looks right without checking the others.

⏱ ANSWER CHOICE FAMILIES

An answer choice family consists of two (in rare cases, three) answer choices that are very similar in construction and cannot all be true at the same time. If you see two answer choices that are direct opposites or parallels, one of them is usually the correct answer. For instance, if one answer choice says that quantity x increases and another either says that quantity x decreases (opposite) or says that quantity y increases (parallel), then those answer choices would fall into the same family. An answer choice that doesn't match the construction of the answer choice family is more likely to be incorrect. Most questions will not have answer choice families, but when they do appear, you should be prepared to recognize them.

⏱ ELIMINATE ANSWERS

Eliminate answer choices as soon as you realize they are wrong, but make sure you consider all possibilities. If you are eliminating answer choices and realize that the last one you are left with is also wrong, don't panic. Start over and consider each choice again. There may be something you missed the first time that you will realize on the second pass.

⏱ AVOID FACT TRAPS

Don't be distracted by an answer choice that is factually true but doesn't answer the question. You are looking for the choice that answers the question. Stay focused on what the question is asking for so you don't accidentally pick an answer that is true but incorrect. Always go back to the question and make sure the answer choice you've selected actually answers the question and is not merely a true statement.

⏱ EXTREME STATEMENTS

In general, you should avoid answers that put forth extreme actions as standard practice or proclaim controversial ideas as established fact. An answer choice that states the "process should be used in certain situations, if..." is much more likely to be correct than one that states the "process should be discontinued completely." The first is a calm rational statement and doesn't even make a definitive, uncompromising stance, using a hedge word *if* to provide wiggle room, whereas the second choice is far more extreme.

✓ BENCHMARK

As you read through the answer choices and you come across one that seems to answer the question well, mentally select that answer choice. This is not your final answer, but it's the one that will help you evaluate the other answer choices. The one that you selected is your benchmark or standard for judging each of the other answer choices. Every other answer choice must be compared to your benchmark. That choice is correct until proven otherwise by another answer choice beating it. If you find a better answer, then that one becomes your new benchmark. Once you've decided that no other choice answers the question as well as your benchmark, you have your final answer.

✓ PREDICT THE ANSWER

Before you even start looking at the answer choices, it is often best to try to predict the answer. When you come up with the answer on your own, it is easier to avoid distractions and traps because you will know exactly what to look for. The right answer choice is unlikely to be word-for-word what you came up with, but it should be a close match. Even if you are confident that you have the right answer, you should still take the time to read each option before moving on.

General Strategies

✓ TOUGH QUESTIONS

If you are stumped on a problem or it appears too hard or too difficult, don't waste time. Move on! Remember though, if you can quickly check for obviously incorrect answer choices, your chances of guessing correctly are greatly improved. Before you completely give up, at least try to knock out a couple of possible answers. Eliminate what you can and then guess at the remaining answer choices before moving on.

✓ CHECK YOUR WORK

Since you will probably not know every term listed and the answer to every question, it is important that you get credit for the ones that you do know. Don't miss any questions through careless mistakes. If at all possible, try to take a second to look back over your answer selection and make sure you've selected the correct answer choice and haven't made a costly careless mistake (such as marking an answer choice that you didn't mean to mark). This quick double check should more than pay for itself in caught mistakes for the time it costs.

✓ PACE YOURSELF

It's easy to be overwhelmed when you're looking at a page full of questions; your mind is confused and full of random thoughts, and the clock is ticking down faster than you would like. Calm down and maintain the pace that you have set for yourself. Especially as you get down to the last few minutes of the test, don't let the small numbers on the clock make you panic. As long as you are on track by monitoring your pace, you are guaranteed to have time for each question.

✓ DON'T RUSH

It is very easy to make errors when you are in a hurry. Maintaining a fast pace in answering questions is pointless if it makes you miss questions that you would have gotten right otherwise. Test writers like to include distracting information and wrong answers that seem right. Taking a little extra time to avoid careless mistakes can make all the difference in your test score. Find a pace that allows you to be confident in the answers that you select.

⊘ KEEP MOVING

Panicking will not help you pass the test, so do your best to stay calm and keep moving. Taking deep breaths and going through the answer elimination steps you practiced can help to break through a stress barrier and keep your pace.

Final Notes

The combination of a solid foundation of content knowledge and the confidence that comes from practicing your plan for applying that knowledge is the key to maximizing your performance on test day. As your foundation of content knowledge is built up and strengthened, you'll find that the strategies included in this chapter become more and more effective in helping you quickly sift through the distractions and traps of the test to isolate the correct answer.

Now that you're preparing to move forward into the test content chapters of this book, be sure to keep your goal in mind. As you read, think about how you will be able to apply this information on the test. If you've already seen sample questions for the test and you have an idea of the question format and style, try to come up with questions of your own that you can answer based on what you're reading. This will give you valuable practice applying your knowledge in the same ways you can expect to on test day.

Good luck and good studying!

Practice Test

Reading

One of the most important skills a person can possess is the ability to read well. Your reading abilities will have an impact on just about every area of your life, in ways that you can't even imagine. People with excellent reading skills will find schoolwork to be much easier. This will be true in all their classes, not just English. If they go on to college, they will be far more likely to make good grades than people who haven't taken the time to develop their reading skills. In the job market, they'll have a powerful advantage over applicants and coworkers whose reading abilities aren't as good as they could be. You should work hard to improve your reading skills in order to get the most out of everything life has to offer.

This part of the assessment will measure your reading comprehension. You'll read a passage, and then answer several questions about it. Don't rush through it; take your time so you can thoroughly understand what you've read. You're not being graded on these exercises, so use them to improve your skills, and to help you prepare for your actual reading tests.

Questions 1 – 12 pertain to the following passage:

ADVENTURE LAND CHASE

(1) I had been waiting for Saturday afternoon for what seemed forever. I had the date circled on the calendar in the kitchen, and my mom even let me cross off the days leading up to it. Every day when I would walk into the kitchen, I would see the date circled in a bright green marker and get even more excited.

(2) Saturday was the day that Adventure Land was opening. It is the largest theme park in three states, has massive rollercoaster's that travel at super speed and loop three times, and has a full water park. But it wasn't just the grand opening of Adventure Land about which I was excited. Saturday was also my best friend Riley's birthday, and to celebrate, she was having her birthday party at Adventure Land.

(3) I woke up very early Saturday morning because I could not sleep. I kept thinking about all the rides that we would go on, the games we were going to play, but more than anything, spending time with all of my friends. While I was eating my cereal, my mom packed us a large bag filled with things she said we were going to need at the theme park all day. She packed sunscreen, sunglasses, and water bottles.

I didn't pay attention, because I was still too excited about the biggest rollercoaster, the Slithering Cobra. It was the one that shot up really high and had three loops. It was going to be so much fun!

(4) When we first got to the park, my first thought was that it was a lot bigger than I thought it was going to be. It was huge! I could see the tops of the rollercoasters from the car in the parking lot. Inside, everything was made to look like a jungle. There were lots of different kinds of trees, both real and fake, there were long green vines draped across the park like telephone lines, and the workers were dressed up as if they were going on safari. The park was so big, and there was so much to do, but then I noticed one huge problem. There were so many people in the park.

Everywhere I looked, there were more people. I was even bumped a few times while we stood at the entrance.

(5) Riley's mom gave all of us wristbands and said that we had to stay with one of our friends at all times.

(6) "Have a buddy," she said. "If anyone gets lost, come to the food court. We will meet at Lickin' Fried Chicken at one o'clock."

(7) Riley was my buddy, and we immediately ran off to go ride the Slithering Cobra.

(8) "Wait up," Charlotte and Ryan called. "We want to come too!"

(9) We stood in line for the ride for over half an hour. There were so many people, and more people kept coming.

(10) "I'm hot," Riley said.

(11) "This is boring," Ryan complained.

(12) When we finally were at the front of the line, the gates opened, and we were allowed to take our seats. Since it was Riley's birthday, they let us ride in the front seats. The rollercoaster took off really fast and went straight into the air. It stopped at the top of the tracks, and it felt as if we were going to fall out of our seats! The rollercoaster tipped over the edge, and soon we were rushing toward the ground. Riley put her arms up, and we both started screaming. The coaster then went straight up and into the three loops. Before we knew it, we were back at the platform, and the ride was over.

(13) "That was awesome!" Charlotte yelled.

(14) "I want to go again!" Ryan added.

(15) We looked at the line, and it had doubled since we had gotten there.

(16) "Maybe later," I said.

(17) When we got off the ride and were walking toward the arcade, our friend Natalie came running up to us. She looked really worried.

(18) "I've lost him," she said. "I lost George! I wasn't supposed to leave him, but I went to the bathroom and now I can't find him!"

(19) "Did you go to the food court?" Ryan asked.

(20) "Yes, and we wasn't there!" she said.

(21) I didn't know what to do. The park was so big, and there were so many people.

(22) "We will have to retrace your steps," Charlotte said. "Where were you the last time you saw him?"

(23) "In the arcade. Playing Skee Ball."

(24) We all started running toward the arcade, which was shaped like a giant tiger.

(25) "Make sure we all stay together!" Ryan called.

(26) It was really hot, and the sun was beating down right on our faces. I probably should have thought about putting on my sunglasses, but all I could think of was George.

(27) "Who is George?" Riley asked me while we were running.

(28) "I thought you knew!" I said. "I have no idea. Maybe her brother?"

(29) It felt really nice to be inside of the arcade. It looked just like a jungle, too. I kept thinking there was no way we were going to find him, but we had to try. We ran up a flight of stairs and across the room to the Skee Ball games.

(30) "There he is!" Natalie pointed forward. We didn't see anything. She ran to one of the alleys and picked up a large stuffed monkey. It was George, the stuffed animal from our homeroom that one student has to take home every weekend and write a story about their adventures. We were bewildered.

(31) "That's the George you were talking about?" Riley whined.

(32) "Of course. Mrs. Miller would have killed me if I lost him! But now I have a great adventure to write about!" she said.

(33) We looked at Natalie and laughed.

(34) "Let's go on another ride," I said, and we all started walking back into the jungle.

1. What is the first reason the narrator gives to explain why she was excited about Saturday?
   a. It was her best friend's birthday
   b. She was going to the beach
   c. Adventure Land was opening
   d. She was going to have the class's stuffed animal

2. In paragraph 3, the author creates a mood of:
   a. Anger
   b. Frustration
   c. Unease
   d. Excitement

3. Paragraphs 1-3 are mainly about:
   a. Why the narrator is looking forward to Saturday
   b. The fun attractions in the narrator's state
   c. Why Adventure Land is fun
   d. Who is coming to the party

4. The narrator uses the words "vines" and "safari" to explain that:

    a. It is hot outside
    b. The theme of the park is the jungle
    c. The park is decorated nicely
    d. The children are not at home

5. Why did Riley's mom ask that every child have a buddy?

    a. So that no one would be lonely
    b. So that no one would get lost
    c. To make the lines for rides move faster
    d. To meet up for lunch

6. Why were the children allowed to ride in the front seat of the rollercoaster?

    a. They had been waiting a really long time
    b. They were in the line for the front seat
    c. They ran and reached the seat the quickest
    d. It was their friend's birthday

7. Why does the narrator discuss the number of people at the park?

    a. To explain why it was important to not get lost
    b. To explain the popularity of the park
    c. To justify her complaints about waiting in line
    d. To explain that it was hot

8. What is the children's main conflict in this selection?

    a. Beating the crowds to get in line for the best ride
    b. Wearing sunscreen
    c. Trying to find a friend they think is lost
    d. Meeting their parents for lunch

9. Why does Ryan ask Natalie if she has been to the food court?

    a. He is hungry and wants to know if the food is good
    b. It is where they were supposed to go if they were lost
    c. It is time to meet up for lunch
    d. He thinks she should talk to one of the parents

10. In paragraph 30, what does the word bewildered mean?

    a. Happy
    b. Upset
    c. Confused
    d. Numb

11. How is the conflict of the story resolved?

    a. The children find George
    b. The lines on the rides become shorter
    c. The children don't care about a stuffed animal
    d. The children leave the park

12. Why are the children surprised at the end of the story?
a. That there were no lines in the arcade
b. Adventure Land was not as much fun as they thought
c. Natalie didn't have a buddy
d. George was a stuffed animal

Questions 13 – 22 pertain to the following passage:

HAPPILY NEVER AFTER

(1) The tragic story of two star-crossed lovers was first brought to attention in William Shakespeare's play, Romeo and Juliet.

(2) The entire plot of the play is explained in the prologue. It is stated that there are two households of equal status in Verona, Italy. There is an ancient feud between the two families that has progressed into the younger generations, meaning the fight between the parents has now become the fight between the parents' children. The narrator continues, saying, "A pair of star-crossed lovers take their life" and in doing so, end their parents' feud. Romeo and Juliet, a child of each household, fall in love, but cannot live happily together because of the feud. The feud is ended, but it is an act that only the death of these children could make happen.

(3) The majority of stories that audiences enjoy have a happy ending. From childhood, people have grown up with the expectation of an ending that comes with the phrase, "And they lived happily ever after." It is interesting that the story of Romeo and Juliet, a famous tragedy, has extreme popularity and interest among both storytellers and audiences. This raises the question of fascination with tragedy.

(4) In the last act of the play, Juliet has faked her death to escape marriage to another man. A message is supposed to be sent to Romeo explaining that she is alive with a plan for their escape. The message, however, does not reach Romeo. In his despair that he has lost his love, he comes to Juliet's side, drinks poison, and dies. Moments later, Juliet wakes up to find Romeo dead. In her grief, she takes his dagger and kills herself.

(5) Within the prologue, the first moments of the play, the audience is told that the main characters die. It is an interesting way of storytelling. The plot has been ruined, and there is no suspense. The audience is told that Romeo and Juliet die, and in doing so, end their parents' feud. The audience, however, remains, and watches the events take place, even though they know the ending and that it will not be happy.

(6) It is therefore logical to assume that audiences want to believe that a story will end happily, even though they are given evidence that it will not. Audiences will watch the entire play, hoping that something will be done so that the lovers can be saved. And yet, as the prologue stated, the message is not delivered, and the only way that Romeo and Juliet can be together is in death. Their deaths had to take place before the ancient feud would end.

(7) The theme of tragic love has been repeated throughout literary history, although perhaps not brought to the extreme of Romeo and Juliet. Although audiences enjoy stories with a happy ending, the popularity of tragic themes proves that audiences

15

also enjoy stories that do not end happily. It is the hope for happiness that gives tragedies strength, and the hope that things will end differently.

13. Which of these sentences is an opinion?
   a. The feud is ended, but it is an act that only the death of their children could make happen
   b. Moments later, Juliet wakes up to find Romeo dead
   c. Audiences will watch the entire play, hoping that something will be done so that the lovers can be saved
   d. It is stated that there are two households of equal status in Verona, Italy

14. What occurs during the first moments of the play?
   a. Romeo dies
   b. There is a fight
   c. Romeo and Juliet share a kiss
   d. The prologue

15. Paragraph 2 helps the reader to understand:
   a. The characters in Romeo and Juliet
   b. The conflict and plot in Romeo and Juliet
   c. The mood and tone in Romeo and Juliet
   d. The theme of Romeo and Juliet

16. What does the word feud mean in paragraph 5?
   a. Fight
   b. Happiness
   c. Sadness
   d. Wealth

17. What is the author's main argument?
   a. Romeo and Juliet is a great play
   b. Audiences will still hope a tragic story will end happily
   c. Tragedies are not as good as stories that have a happy ending
   d. Prologues should not ruin the story

18. What does the word evidence mean in paragraph 6?
   a. Hope
   b. Questions
   c. Proof
   d. Sadness

19. Why does the author use the phrase, "And they lived happily ever after"?
   a. To explain that most audiences enjoy stories with a happy ending
   b. To explain the ending of Romeo and Juliet
   c. To explain why happy endings are not as good as tragic endings
   d. To explain how to end a story

20. The author explains that Romeo believes Juliet to be dead because:
   a. He watched her take his dagger
   b. She drank poison
   c. She was ill on her wedding day
   d. He never received the message explaining that she faked her death

21. Why does the author think that the prologue in Romeo and Juliet is "an interesting way of storytelling"?
   a. The prologue explains that the play is a tragedy
   b. The prologue explains how the story will end
   c. The prologue is very long
   d. The prologue asks the audience a question

22. Why, according to the prologue and author, are Romeo and Juliet's deaths necessary?
   a. To make the play a tragedy
   b. To show the dangers of poison
   c. To end their parents' feud
   d. To earn more money and power

Questions 23 – 25 pertain to the following poem:

THE WINDOW

Rain spilled like rivers—

the wind whispered

against the window.

Steam rose from the cup

in swirls;

white against the darkness.

Nestled in the warmth

of blankets and tea,

Mother listened to the sounds

knocking outside the window.

23. In the poem, "The Window," what is an example of personification?
   a. Spilled
   b. Nestled
   c. Whispered
   d. Rose

24. In the poem, "The Window," the author uses a simile to compare:

a. Steam and swirls
b. Blankets and tea
c. White and darkness
d. Rain and rivers

25. In the poem, "The Window," what is a proper noun?

a. Nestled
b. Mother
c. Rain
d. darkness

Questions 26 – 33 pertain to the following passage:

MUSICALLY INCLINED

(1) Gibson thought, at least, that it could have been worse. His parents could have named him Fender, given him the middle name Les Paul, or worse yet, Stratocaster. This was a small comfort to him as he reminded himself that he really never had a chance. It was not he who chose the music. He was born into it, and even named after one of the most famous guitars. It was like the music had found him.

(2) Gibson could not remember a time when he did not know how to play music. His mother was a singer when she was younger, and his father played the lead guitar in the band Mookie Harper. Growing up, he learned to read music at the same time he learned to read words. Music felt as natural to him as walking and was a big part of his life.

(3) There were many instruments in Gibson's house, and over the years, he had learned how to play most of them. He started with a piano when he was very young, moved to the harmonica and drums when he was a bit older, and had just begun learning how to play the violin. But Gibson's favorite instrument was the one he had been playing the longest: his father's Gibson Les Paul guitar.

(4) At school, Gibson felt lonely most days. His family had just moved from Seattle, and the other kids at school thought it was weird that he carried a violin case to school for his fourth period music class. At his old school, he was in the school band, and had a lot of friends who enjoyed playing music with him.

(5) "Why would you play the violin?" Joe asked as he snickered in his chair. "Only girls play that. I bet it was the only thing you could learn," he laughed. The rest of the class laughed behind him.

(6) Gibson sat in his chair and rolled his eyes. He thought that this kid obviously didn't know anything about music, because the violin was one of the most challenging instruments to learn. He left the case on the floor by his chair and waited for his second period history class to begin.

(7) The teacher walked into the classroom pushing a cart. Gibson immediately sat up in his chair. He knew exactly what was in the cases and smiled.

(8) "I was able to borrow these from the music section of the museum to show you today," Ms. Conway said. "Can anyone tell me what these are?" she asked.

(9) "They are guitars, Ms. Conway. Duh," Joe, a boy in the back of the room, said. The class laughed.

(10) Ms. Conway squinted her eyes at Joe. "He is half right," she said. "These are in fact guitars. But can anyone tell me what kind of guitars they are?" She looked around the room. Everyone sat still.

(11) "The one on the right is a 1958 Gibson Les Paul," Gibson said out of the silence. "And the one of the left is a vintage Fender Stratocaster from 1954. Oh, and they are electric guitars," he said.

(12) The class looked at Gibson and stared in silence. Ms. Conway clapped her hands together. "Wow! You're right, Gibson. Great job!"

(13) "How'd you know that?" a girl asked behind him.

(14) "My dad has both of them," he said. "And I've been playing them since I was little."

(15) "You can play the guitar?" Joe laughed. "Yeah right! You play the violin!" He looked around, but no one else was laughing.

(16) "Would you like to play something?" Ms. Conway asked. Gibson looked down at his feet. He didn't know what to say. He just wanted to stay in his seat and have no one look at him.

(17) But then he thought of his dad and smiled. "I'll play the Les Paul," he said. "It's my favorite."

(18) He walked toward the front of the class and picked up the guitar. He played the opening notes of "Gone into the Sun." It was his favorite Mookie Harper song. All of the children sat in awe as they watched him play, and when he was done, they all started clapping and cheering.

(19) "Maybe I'll start playing the violin," the boy next to him said. "If it will get me to play a guitar like that!"

26. Paragraphs 1 through 3 are mainly about:
a. How music has inspired Gibson's family and his life
b. How Gibson will be in a band one day
c. How Gibson wanted to be named after a Fender guitar
d. Why Gibson is moving schools

27. This story is told in what point of view?
a. First-person limited
b. First-person omniscient
c. Third-person omniscient
d. Third-person limited

28. Why did the narrator include the detail that the family was from Seattle?

   a. To show why the family loves music
   b. To show that Gibson was a new student
   c. To show that the family moves a lot because of the father's band
   d. To show that the family is on vacation

29. What does Gibson mean when he assumes that he "never really had a chance?"

   a. That he was destined to play music because of his family and his name
   b. That he was never going to be good at playing the violin
   c. That he was never going to be popular at school
   d. That he is going to be in a band one day like his father

30. What instrument had Gibson been playing the longest?

   a. Violin
   b. Harmonica
   c. Les Paul guitar
   d. Fender Stratocaster guitar

31. In paragraph 16, why did Gibson want to sit in his seat?

   a. He did not like the guitar and did not want to play it
   b. He did not want the attention of the other children to be on him
   c. He wanted to play the violin instead
   d. He thought the guitar was too old to play

32. The author arranges this selection by:

   a. Explaining how Gibson grew to like to play the violin
   b. Showing how Gibson taught his classmates how to play guitar
   c. Listing why the children laughed at Gibson
   d. Describing how his love for music helped Gibson be himself at school

33. How is the internal conflict in the story resolved?

   a. Gibson is himself and is liked by his classmates
   b. Gibson decides not to play in front of everyone
   c. Gibson decides to start a band with people in his class
   d. Gibson plays a song for his dad

Questions 34 – 42 pertain to the following essay that Timmy has written on why he feels books will soon be a thing of the past:

THE INVENTIONS OF TECHNOLOGY

(1) Stories have been a part of the world since the beginning of recorded time. For centuries before the invention of the printing press, stories of the world were passed down to generations through oral tradition. With the invention of the printing press, which made written material available to wide ranges of audiences, books were mass-produced and introduced into greater society.

(2) For the last several centuries, books have been at the forefront of education and entertainment. With the invention of the Internet, reliance on books for information quickly changed. Soon, almost everything that anyone needed to know could be

accessed through the Internet. Large, printed volumes of encyclopedias became unnecessary as all of the information was easily available on the Internet.

(3) Despite the progression of the Internet, printed media was still very popular in the forms of both fiction and non-fiction books. While waiting for an appointment, enduring a several-hour flight, or relaxing before sleep, books have been a reliable and convenient source of entertainment, and one that society has not been willing to give up.

(4) With the progression and extreme convenience of technology, printed books are going to soon become a thing of the past. Inventions such as the iPad from Macintosh and the Kindle have made the need for any kind of printed media unnecessary. With a rechargeable battery, a large screen, and the ability to have several books saved on file, electronic options will soon take over and society will no longer see printed books.

(5) Although some people may say that the act of reading is not complete without turning a page, sliding a finger across the screen or pressing a button to read more onto the next page is just as satisfying to the reader. The iPad and Kindle are devices that have qualities similar to a computer and can be used for so much more than just reading. These devices are therefore better than books because they have multiple uses.

(6) In a cultural society that is part of the world and due to a longstanding tradition, stories will always be an important way to communicate ideas and provide information and entertainment. Centuries ago, stories could only be remembered and retold through speech. Printed media changed the way the world communicated and was connected, and now, as we move forward with technology, it is only a matter of time before we must say goodbye to the printed past and welcome the digital and electronic future.

34. What is the main argument of this essay?
   a. iPad and Kindles are easier to read than books
   b. The printing press was a great invention
   c. The Internet is how people receive information
   d. Technology will soon replace printed material

35. What is the main purpose of paragraph 1?
   a. To explain oral tradition
   b. To explain the importance of the printing press
   c. To explain the progression of stories within society
   d. To introduce the essay

36. What does the word enduring mean in paragraph 3?
   a. Quitting
   b. Undergo
   c. Sleeping
   d. Thriving

37. According to the essay, what was the first way that stories were communicated and passed down?

   a. Oral tradition
   b. Printed books
   c. Technology
   d. Hand writing

38. According to the essay, what changed the reliance on books?

   a. Inventions such as the iPad
   b. The printing press
   c. The Internet
   d. Volumes of encyclopedias

39. Which of the following statements is an opinion?

   a. Despite the progression of the Internet, printed media was still very popular in the forms of both fiction and non-fiction books
   b. Although some people may say that the act of reading is not complete without turning a page, sliding a finger across the screen or pressing a button to read more onto the next page is just as satisfying to the reader
   c. With the invention of the Internet, reliance on books for information quickly changed
   d. Stories have been a part of the world since the beginning of recorded time

40. What is a secondary argument the author makes?

   a. Devices such as the iPad or Kindle are better than books because they have multiple uses
   b. Books are still important to have while waiting for an appointment or taking a flight
   c. Printed encyclopedias are still used and more convenient that using the Internet
   d. With technology, there will soon be no need for stories

41. How is the essay organized?

   a. The author explains details as to why he wants to have an iPad
   b. The author explains how stories eventually let into oral tradition
   c. The author explains technology to explain why books are not needed
   d. The author explains the history of stories within society and the ways they progress with time

42. Which of the following statements is not an example of a categorical claim?

   a. With a rechargeable battery, a large screen, and the ability to have several books saved on file, electronic options will soon take over and society will no longer see printed books.
   b. Soon, almost everything that anyone needed to know could be accessed through the Internet.
   c. The iPad and Kindle are devices that have qualities similar to a computer and can be used for so much more than just reading.
   d. With the progression and extreme convenience of technology, printed books are going to soon become a thing of the past.

Questions 43 – 50 pertain to the following passage:

THE EDUCATIONAL MARKET TOWN

(1) Aberystwyth is a market town on the West Coast of Wales within the United Kingdom. A market town refers to European areas that have the right to have

markets, which differentiates it from a city or village. The town is located where two rivers meet, the River Ystwyth and River Rheidol and is the best known as an educational center, housing an established university since 1872.

(2) The town is situated between North Wales and South Wales, and is a large vacation destination as well as tourist attraction. Constitution Hill is a hill on the north end of Aberystwyth, which provides excellent views of Cardigan Bay and which is supported by the Aberystwyth Electric Cliff Railway. Although Aberystwyth is known as a modern Welsh town, it is home to several historic buildings, such as the remnants of a castle.

(3) Although there are several grocery, clothing, sporting goods, and various other miscellaneous shops, Aberystwyth is best known for its educational services. Aberystwyth University, formerly known as University College Wales, as well as the National Library of Wales, which is the legal deposit library for Wales and which houses all Welsh publications, are both located within Aberystwyth. The two main languages traditionally spoken in Aberystwyth are English and Welsh. With local live music, arts center, and educational opportunities in gorgeous scenery, Aberystwyth is a hidden luxury within the United Kingdom.

43. Where is Aberystwyth located?
  a. England
  b. Ireland
  c. Scotland
  d. Wales

44. What is the purpose of this essay?
  a. To explain that the university was established in 1872
  b. To explain the legal deposit library in Wales
  c. To provide a portrait of a town
  d. To explain the views in Aberystwyth

45. What does the word situated mean in paragraph 2?
  a. located
  b. fighting
  c. luxurious
  d. hidden

46. Which of the following statements is an opinion?
  a. Although Aberystwyth is known as a modern Welsh town, it is home to several historic buildings, such as the remnants of a castle
  b. With local live music, arts center, and educational opportunities in gorgeous scenery, Aberystwyth is a hidden luxury within the United Kingdom
  c. The two main languages traditionally spoken in Aberystwyth are English and Welsh
  d. Aberystwyth is a market town on the West Coast of Wales within the United Kingdom

47. How many languages are traditionally spoken in Aberystwyth?

    a. One
    b. Two
    c. Three
    d. More than three

48. What makes Aberystwyth a market town?

    a. It is a city
    b. It is a village
    c. It has the right to have a market
    d. There are markets in town every day

49. What is Constitution Hill supported by?

    a. Cardigan Bay
    b. The ocean
    c. North Wales
    d. Aberystwyth Electric Cliff Railway

50. What is Aberystwyth best known as?

    a. An educational center
    b. A market town
    c. A music center
    d. A hiking center

Written Expression

Expressing yourself well in written communications is just as important today as it ever was, even though text messaging has become the preferred form of communication for tens of millions of young people. While it's fun to use acronyms, slang, and emoticons to express yourself when you're dealing with your friends and family members, that sort of communication isn't at all appropriate in the workplace, or in other situations requiring the use of proper English. You'll want to know the rules and principles of Written Expression so well that they become second nature. Here are some exercises to help you improve in this area.

Questions 1 – 5 are based on the following:

She Walks in Beauty

by Lord Byron

She walks in beauty, like the night

Of cloudless climes and starry skies;

And all that's best of dark and bright

Meet in her aspect and her eyes:

Thus mellowed to that tender light

Which heaven to gaudy day denies.

One shade the more, one ray the less,

Had half impaired the nameless grace

Which waves in every raven tress,

Or softly lightens o'er her face;

Where thoughts serenely sweet express

How pure, how dear their dwelling-place.

And on that cheek, and o'er that brow,

So soft, so calm, yet eloquent,

The smiles that win, the tints that glow,

But tell of days in goodness spent,

A mind at peace with all below,

A heart whose love is innocent!

1. The following lines refer to what characteristic of the woman being talked about in the poem?

> Where thoughts serenely sweet express
> How pure, how dear their dwelling-place

a. her hair
b. her eyes
c. her mind
d. her face

2. The rhyme scheme of this poem is

a. ABABAB, CDCDCD, efefeF.
b. ABABBA, CDCDDC, EFEFFE.
c. ABAABB, CDCCDD, EFEEFF.
d. ABCBCA, CDEDEC, EFCFCE.

3. The following line contains an example of which poetic device?

> Of cloudless climes and starry skies

a. personification
b. rhyming couplet
c. alliteration
d. quatrain

4. The images of darkness and light in this poem can be interpreted as showing

a. that beauty doesn't last and you should enjoy it whenever you encounter it.
b. how people view beauty differently at different times in their lives.
c. how something that is beautiful may look different at different times and under different circumstances, but always remains beautiful.
d. the speaker's devotion to the woman he is praising.

5. This poem was inspired by Byron's cousin's wife, Anne Beatrix Wilmot, whom he observed at a party one night. Byron's friend James W. Webster witnessed his friend's reaction, and is quoted as saying:

> "When we returned to his [Byron's] rooms in Albany (after the party), he said little, but desired Fletcher to give him a tumbler of brandy, which he drank at once to Mrs. Wilmot's health, then retired to rest, and was, I heard afterwards, in a sad state all night. The next day he wrote those charming lines upon her—She walks in Beauty like the Night..."

How would this information likely influence a reader's interpretation of the poem?

a. Knowing that this poem is based on observations of a married woman changes the context of what the author is saying and what it may mean.
b. It would make the reader dislike the woman being talked about in the poem.
c. Knowing who the poem is about provides clarification as to the season during which the poem takes place.
d. It makes it easier to identify the speaker of the poem.

The following is an excerpt from The House of Mirth *by Edith Wharton. This novel tells the tragic tale of Lily Bart, a beautiful woman who lives the life of a socialite, even though she herself has no money, and must marry in order to maintain the lifestyle to which she has become accustomed. To do this, she must maintain her reputation as a desirable catch for wealthy suitors.*

In the hansom she leaned back with a sigh. Why must a girl pay so dearly for her least escape from routine? Why could one never do a natural thing without having to screen it behind a structure of artifice? She had yielded to a passing impulse in going to Lawrence Selden's rooms, and it was so seldom that she could allow herself the luxury of an impulse! This one, at any rate, was going to cost her rather more than she could afford. She was vexed to see that, in spite of so many years of vigilance, she had blundered twice within five minutes. That stupid story about her dress-maker was bad enough—it would have been so simple to tell Rosedale that she had been taking tea with Selden! The mere statement of the fact would have rendered it innocuous. But, after having let herself be surprised in a falsehood, it was doubly stupid to snub the witness of her discomfiture. If she had had the presence of mind to let Rosedale drive her to the station, the concession might have purchased his silence. He had his race's accuracy in the appraisal of values, and to be seen walking down the platform at the crowded afternoon hour in the company of Miss Lily Bart would have been money in his pocket, as he might himself have phrased it. He knew, of course, that there would be a large house-party at Bellomont, and the possibility of being taken for one of Mrs. Trenor's guests was doubtless included in his calculations. Mr. Rosedale was still at a stage in his social ascent when it was of importance to produce such impressions.

The provoking part was that Lily knew all this—knew how easy it would have been to silence him on the spot, and how difficult it might be to do so afterward. Mr. Simon Rosedale was a man who made it his business to know everything about every one, whose idea of showing himself to be at home in society was to display an inconvenient familiarity with the habits of those with whom he wished to be thought intimate. Lily was sure that within twenty-four hours the story of her visiting her dress-maker at the Benedick would be in active circulation among Mr. Rosedale's acquaintances. The worst of it was that she had always snubbed and ignored him. On his first appearance—when her improvident cousin, Jack Stepney, had obtained for him (in return for favours too easily guessed) a card to one of the vast impersonal Van Osburgh "crushes"—Rosedale, with that mixture of artistic sensibility and business astuteness which characterizes his race, had instantly gravitated toward Miss Bart. She understood his motives, for her own course was guided by as nice calculations. Training and experience had taught her to be hospitable to newcomers, since the most unpromising might be useful later on, and there were plenty of available oubliettes to swallow them if they were not. But some intuitive repugnance, getting the better of years of social discipline, had made her push Mr. Rosedale into his oubliette without a trial. He had left behind only the ripple of amusement which his speedy dispatch had caused among her friends; and though later (to shift the metaphor) he reappeared lower down the stream, it was only in fleeting glimpses, with long submergences between.

Hitherto Lily had been undisturbed by scruples. In her little set Mr. Rosedale had been pronounced "impossible," and Jack Stepney roundly snubbed for his attempt to pay his debts in dinner invitations. Even Mrs. Trenor, whose taste for variety had led her into some hazardous experiments, resisted Jack's attempts to disguise Mr. Rosedale as a novelty, and declared that he was the same little Jew who had been served up and rejected at the social board a dozen times within her memory; and while Judy Trenor was obdurate there was small chance of Mr. Rosedale's penetrating beyond the outer limbo of the Van Osburgh crushes. Jack gave up the contest with a laughing "You'll see," and, sticking manfully to his guns, showed himself with Rosedale at the fashionable restaurants, in company with the personally vivid if socially obscure ladies who are available for such purposes. But the attempt had hitherto been vain, and as Rosedale undoubtedly paid for the dinners, the laugh remained with his debtor.

Mr. Rosedale, it will be seen, was thus far not a factor to be feared—unless one put one's self in his power. And this was precisely what Miss Bart had done. Her clumsy fib had let him see that she had something to conceal; and she was sure he had a score to settle with her. Something in his smile told her he had not forgotten. She turned from the thought with a little shiver, but it hung on her all the way to the station, and dogged her down the platform with the persistency of Mr. Rosedale himself.

6. Why does Lily worry about how Mr. Rosedale will interpret his run-in with her outside of Selden's apartment building?
    a. She is afraid that he will spread rumors that she has been acting improperly, and that these rumors may have a negative effect on her social position.
    b. She is afraid that he will think less of her because she lied.
    c. She is worried that Rosedale will try to convince her to be his wife.
    d. She is looking to begin a relationship with Rosedale.

7. This passage is told from whose point of view?
    a. Simon Rosedale
    b. Lily Bart
    c. Jack Stepney
    d. Lawrence Selden

8. In the film version of *The House of Mirth*, this scene is portrayed by three actors. The audience observes Lily, Selden, and Rosedale meeting outside the Benedick, and watches the events that unfold. This change of medium makes analyzing the events through Lily's thoughts impossible, so much of the back story presented in the text is lost in the film version. What detail would most likely be missed by telling the story through the medium of film?
    a. Lily does not like Rosedale, but will keep up the pretenses of being sociable and polite to him in public.
    b. Lily is uncomfortable with the situation she is in.
    c. Lily lied about her reason for being at the Benedick.
    d. Rosedale has ulterior motives for offering Lily a ride.

9. What does "sticking manfully to his guns" mean as it is used in this passage?
   a. Jack Stepney could easily turn violent in the face of society's rejection of Rosedale.
   b. Rosedale is continuing to persist in his efforts to break into Lily's circle of friends, but is becoming discouraged by their constant rejection of him.
   c. Rosedale is optimistic that if he persists in his efforts to break into Lily's circle of friends, he will eventually be successful.
   d. Jack Stepney is standing behind his public support of Rosedale in important social circles, despite the fact that important members of society have snubbed them both for it.

10. References to Rosedale's "race" and lines such as "that he was the same little Jew who had been served up and rejected at the social board a dozen times within her memory" reveal what about Lily's set of friends?
   a. They are envious of Rosedale's success and charisma.
   b. They are afraid of Rosedale because of his family lineage.
   c. They are discriminating against Rosedale because he is Jewish.
   d. They are mistaken about where Rosedale's wealth came from.

"The Gettysburg Address" was a speech given by President Abraham Lincoln on Nov. 19, 1863 at the dedication of the Gettysburg National Cemetery, the final resting place of soldiers killed in the Battle of Gettysburg during the Civil War.

The Gettysburg Address

Four score and seven years ago our fathers brought forth, upon this continent, a new nation, conceived in Liberty, and dedicated to the proposition that all men are created equal.

Now we are engaged in a great civil war, testing whether that nation, or any nation so conceived, and so dedicated, can long endure. We are met here on a great battlefield of that war. We have come to dedicate a portion of it as a final resting place for those who here gave their lives that that nation might live. It is altogether fitting and proper that we should do this.

But in a larger sense we cannot dedicate - we cannot consecrate - we cannot hallow this ground. The brave men, living and dead, who struggled here, have consecrated it far above our poor power to add or detract. The world will little note, nor long remember, what we say here, but can never forget what they did here.

It is for us, the living, rather to be dedicated here to the unfinished work which they have, thus far, so nobly carried on. It is rather for us to be here dedicated to the great task remaining before us - that from these honored dead we take increased devotion to that cause for which they here gave the last full measure of devotion - that we here highly resolve that these dead shall not have died in vain; that this nation shall have a new birth of freedom; and that this government of the people, by the people, for the people, shall not perish from the earth.

11. What is the main message of this speech?

a. Those who died in this battle honor this land we are dedicating today better than anyone else.

b. As we honor those who died in this battle, we should move forward with renewed dedication to ensuring the nation our founding fathers created continues to function the way they intended.

c. We need to put the regrets of the past aside, without remembering the sacrifices of those who gave their lives for our country.

d. The war we are fighting is far from over, as evidenced by the number of lives lost in this battle.

12. The phrase "the world will little note" means what?

a. The world will not soon forget.

b. The world will record what we say here.

c. The world will not pay much attention.

d. The world will recall what we do with perfect accuracy.

13. There were nearly 100 years between the American Revolution and the Civil War. The speech connects ideas about these two conflicts by saying that the ideas of the Civil War

a. threaten those of the Revolution.

b. are similar to those of the Revolution.

c. are newer than those of the Revolution.

d. are better than those of the Revolution.

14. Why does Lincoln most likely talk about the past before he talks about the present?

a. to incite listeners of his message to protest

b. to remember what has been lost in the past

c. to establish context for his main message

d. to try to get listeners to side with his position

15. What is the following sentence addressing?

Now we are engaged in a great civil war, testing whether that nation, or any nation so conceived, and so dedicated, can long endure.

a. whether or not a nation based on ideas of freedom and equality can survive for any significant length of time

b. whether or not the Union will be able to preserve the existing structure of the United States by preventing the Confederacy from seceding

c. whether or not the Confederacy will be successful in seceding from the United States and surviving on its own

d. whether or not Lincoln should continue dedicating troops to the war

The following is an excerpt from "Love," an essay written by noted transcendentalist author Ralph Waldo Emerson. It appears in his collection Essays, First Series, *which was published in 1841.*

V. Love

I was as a gem concealed;

Me my burning ray revealed.

> —Koran.

Every promise of the soul has innumerable fulfillments; each of its joys ripens into a new want. Nature, uncontainable, flowing, forelooking, in the first sentiment of kindness anticipates already a benevolence which shall lose all particular regards in its general light. The introduction to this felicity is in a private and tender relation of one to one, which is the enchantment of human life; which, like a certain divine rage and enthusiasm, seizes on man at one period and works a revolution in his mind and body; unites him to his race, pledges him to the domestic and civic relations, carries him with new sympathy into nature, enhances the power of the senses, opens the imagination, adds to his character heroic and sacred attributes, establishes marriage, and gives permanence to human society.

The natural association of the sentiment of love with the heyday of the blood seems to require that in order to portray it in vivid tints, which every youth and maid should confess to be true to their throbbing experience, one must not be too old. The delicious fancies of youth reject the least savor of a mature philosophy, as chilling with age and pedantry their purple bloom. And therefore I know I incur the imputation of unnecessary hardness and stoicism from those who compose the Court and Parliament of Love. But from these formidable censors I shall appeal to my seniors. For it is to be considered that this passion of which we speak, though it begin with the young, yet forsakes not the old, or rather suffers no one who is truly its servant to grow old, but makes the aged participators of it not less than the tender maiden, though in a different and nobler sort. For it is a fire that kindling its first embers in the narrow nook of a private bosom, caught from a wandering spark out of another private heart, glows and enlarges until it warms and beams upon multitudes of men and women, upon the universal heart of all, and so lights up the whole world and all nature with its generous flames. It matters not therefore whether we attempt to describe the passion at twenty, at thirty, or at eighty years. He who paints it at the first period will lose some of its later, he who paints it at the last, some of its earlier traits. Only it is to be hoped that by patience and the Muses' aid we may attain to that inward view of the law which shall describe a truth ever young and beautiful, so central that it shall commend itself to the eye, at whatever angle beholden.

And the first condition is, that we must leave a too close and lingering adherence to facts, and study the sentiment as it appeared in hope and not in history. For each man sees his own life defaced and disfigured, as the life of man is not, to his imagination. Each man sees over his own experience a certain stain of error, whilst that of other men looks fair and ideal. Let any man go back to those delicious relations which make the beauty of his life, which have given him sincerest instruction and nourishment, he will shrink and moan. Alas! I know not why, but infinite compunctions embitter in mature life the remembrances of budding joy and cover every beloved name. Everything is beautiful seen from the point of the intellect, or as truth. But all is sour, if seen as experience. Details are melancholy; the plan is seemly and noble. In the actual world—the painful kingdom of time and place—dwell care, and canker, and fear. With thought, with the ideal, is immortal hilarity, the rose of joy. Round it all the Muses sing. But grief cleaves to names, and persons, and the partial interests of to-day and yesterday.

16. In the first paragraph, Emerson says that
    a. love unites and gives endurance to human society.
    b. the search for love is the main pursuit of life.
    c. a life without love is one that is unfulfilled.
    d. none of the above

17. When Emerson references "the heyday of the blood" in the second paragraph, he is talking about
    a. energy.
    b. spirit.
    c. youth.
    d. arrogance.

18. To what is Emerson referring in the following sentence?

For it is a fire that kindling its first embers in the narrow nook of a private bosom, caught from a wandering spark out of another private heart, glows and enlarges until it warms and beams upon multitudes of men and women, upon the universal heart of all, and so lights up the whole world and all nature with its generous flames.

    a. age
    b. love
    c. health
    d. time

19. What is Emerson's explanation for why people think that others' lives are better or more fulfilled than theirs?
    a. Ignorance is bliss. People would rather live out their fantasies through the lives of others instead of facing the risk of finding out that reality isn't all that it is cracked up to be.
    b. You can't always get what you want. We may desire better, more fulfilled lives, but few are able to do what is necessary to achieve this goal. This causes bitterness and resentment.
    c. Truth is stranger than fiction. What happens in reality is often more detailed and stranger than what is made up by the mind.
    d. Ideas are better than reality. While there is always a possibility that an idea or a fantasy could come true, the reality of experience proves that the idea of something is much different from and usually better than the reality.

20. The following sentence is the thesis of Grant Allen's 1889 essay "Falling in Love." How does Grant's approach to discussing love differ from Emerson's?

> In short, my doctrine is simply the old-fashioned and confiding belief that marriages are made in heaven: with the further corollary that heaven manages them, one time with another, a great deal better than Sir George Campbell.

a. Grant discusses how love leads to the destruction of society; Emerson addresses how it helps build societies.

b. Grant discusses how love has affected his life; Emerson addresses how love has affected the lives of others.

c. Grant discusses the reason love exists; Emerson addresses times when love was not valued in society.

d. Grant discusses the idea of love as it relates to marriage; Emerson addresses the effects of love on the individual and on society as a whole.

Joey wanted to learn more about the U.S. Coast Guard, and chose it as his topic when his teacher asked each student to write an informational essay. A draft of his essay follows.

(1) The United States Coast Guard was founded in 1790 as the branch of military service responsible for safeguarding the country's sea-related interests. (2) It was originally created to protect the U.S. from smugglers, and to enforce tariff and trade laws. (3) It may seem like this would be a job for the Navy, but the purpose of the Navy is very different from that of the Coast Guard. (4) The Navy's job is to engage in combat and defend the seas from threats to the U.S. and its interests worldwide. (5) The Coast Guard is actually a part of the Department of Homeland Security, and is considered a federal law enforcement agency. (6) Its mission is to protect and enforce laws on our coastlines and in our ports, and to safeguard other interests within American waters.

(7) In addition to its role as a maritime law enforcement agency, the Coast Guard also serves as a guardian of the environment. (8) This includes stopping waste and other types of pollution from being dumped into the ocean, preventing and helping to clean up oil spills, and even ensuring that species of marine life that could threaten the balance of existing environments are prevented from being introduced. (9) This is a very important job for the Coast Guard, because there would not be much of a coastline to protect if our seas were too polluted to enjoy and sustain us.

(10) On the whole, Coast Guard personnel perform the following in a single day: save 12 lives; respond to 64 search and rescue cases; keep 842 pounds of cocaine off the streets; service 116 buoys and fix 24 discrepancies; screen 720 commercial vessels, and 183,000 crew and passengers; issue 173 credentials to merchant mariners; investigate 13 marine accidents; inspect 68 containers and 29 vessels for compliance with air emissions standards; perform 28 safety and environmental examinations of foreign vessels; board 13 fishing boats to ensure compliance with fisheries laws; and respond and investigate 10 pollution incidents.

(11) In addition to the day-to-day role of the Coast Guard, this branch of service also plays an important role in many large-scale and humanitarian operations. (12) In 2010, the Coast Guard launched a mission to provide assistance directly following the devastating earthquake in Haiti. (13) It was there in response

to the *Deepwater Horizon* explosion that caused the dumping of millions of gallons of crude oil in to the Gulf of Mexico. (14) It was there to seize $80 million worth of cocaine out of the hands of smugglers.

21. **Which paragraph establishes the subject and context of this article?**
    a. paragraph 1
    b. paragraph 2
    c. paragraph 3
    d. paragraph 4

22. **Which of the following sentences, if placed before sentence 10, would create a better transition from the second paragraph to the third paragraph?**
    a. The "Coastie" life is one that just about anyone would want to choose.
    b. The life of a Coast Guard member (or "Coastie") can be routine and boring, depending on what type of job the "Coastie" has.
    c. There are many things that the Coast Guard can do to enforce laws while at sea or patrolling our waterways.
    d. Enforcement of laws and protection of the environment are just two of the many responsibilities that a member of the Coast Guard (or "Coastie") can expect to have in the line of duty.

23. **Adding which of the following sentences to paragraph 3 would make it more credible?**
    a. This information comes from the official Coast Guard Web site.
    b. The average age of Coast Guard members is 28.
    c. The Coast Guard has a long history of service.
    d. There are 33,200 enlisted Coast Guard members.

24. **Which of the following would be the best conclusion for this essay?**
    a. There is much more that we can learn about the Coast Guard. To list all of the great things about this organization would take all day. The opportunities available to members of the Coast Guard are endless, and we should all consider becoming a "Coastie."
    b. Being a "Coastie" would be the fulfillment of anyone's dreams. Who wouldn't want a career that is full of adventure and honor? There is no better job that a person could pursue as their life's work.
    c. The Coast Guard is a very diverse and exciting branch of the U.S. military. Though many may not believe it is as important as the Navy, the Army, the Marines, or the Air Force, it's plain to see that the Coast Guard plays a vital role in ensuring our nation's security and prosperity.
    d. The Coast Guard provides little support toward defending our nation from threats, as its members are always so close to home. Greater purpose can be found in a different branch of service. The threats that the Coast Guard faces are insignificant when compared to those faced by the Army, the Navy, the Marines, or the Air Force.

25. Joey wants to publish his essay online so that his grandmother can see it. What would be the fastest way for him to do this?

   a. He should try to convince his local newspaper to publish it in its online edition, and then send his grandmother the link.
   b. He should try to convince his school newspaper to publish it, and then scan a copy of it into a computer and send the file to his grandmother.
   c. He should work with the school's A/V department to record a copy of him reading the essay, post the file on the school's Web site, and then send his grandmother the link.
   d. He should publish the essay as a blog post, and then send his grandmother the link.

26. Joey's teacher likes his essay, but wants him to revise it so that it focuses more on the role of the Coast Guard in U.S. history. Which of the following would be the best place for him to look to find out what the Coast Guard did to protect our shores during World War II?

   a. *The* Greatest Battles of WWII documentary from the History Channel
   b. An article entitled "U.S. Coast Guard Combat Victories of World War II" on the official Coast Guard Web site
   c. An entry entitled "World War II" found in the Encyclopedia Britannica
   d. An article entitled "History of the United States Navy" found on Wikipedia

Brett was asked to write a short narrative about his most memorable experience. A draft of his essay follows.

(1) My most memorable experience was meeting my baby sister for the first time. (2) Though I knew that my mom was pregnant, I don't think I was really aware of what that meant and how it would change my life until I saw Megan's little face for the very first time.

(3) I loved my mom and dad. (4) I loved my life. (5) I loved being the center of their attention. (6) Playing with Mom and Dad was the best. (7) As my mom began to get bigger, though, she couldn't play with me as much. (8) I couldn't understand why she was so tired all of the time, or why she couldn't run around with me at the soccer field like she used to. (9) My dad said that it was because of the new baby that was inside of her. (10) That was when I started to hate the baby.

(11) Who was she to take so much energy from my mom and prevent her from playing with me? (12) Why were my parents so concerned about this kid that wasn't even here yet, and what would happen when she got here? (13) Did all of this mean that I would always get the short end of the stick?

(14) I started to worry that once the baby came, my parents would forget all about me. (15) The baby would be the only thing they thought about, the only thing they cared about. (16) I would get lost in the shuffle because I wasn't their only child anymore.

(17) You can imagine how upset I was the day my mom went into labor, and my parents sent me to stay with my grandma until the baby was born. (18) Everything I'd been fearing and stressing about for months was about to come true. (19) Thinking back, I'm really embarrassed that I threw a tantrum and added to my parents' difficulties that day. (20) I was scared, though. (21) I thought I was losing the two most important people in my life.

35

(22) I didn't want to go to the hospital to see my new baby sister, but my grandma made me go. (23) I'm so glad she did. (24) When we got to my mom's room, my dad came out and gave me the biggest hug I'd ever gotten.

(25) "Hey, big brother," he said. (26) "Ready to meet the person who is going to think you are the coolest person in the world?"

(27) When I saw my mom, she handed the baby to my dad and held out her arms to me. (28) I crawled onto her bed and hugged her as hard as I could. (29) Though I knew she was in pain from her C-section, she still stroked my hair and whispered "I love you, baby" in my ear. (30) She made a place for me on her lap, and then cradled the baby so that I could see her little face for the first time.

(31) "Megan, meet the best big brother that anyone could ask for," my mom said to the baby.

(32) I knew then that nothing would come between my parents and me. (33) They could pour all of their love into me and still have enough love for my little sister. (34) And I learned that I had enough love in me for a new member of our family, too. (35) As Baby Megan slept quietly in my mom's arms, her little hand grabbed onto my finger and squeezed it tight, like I was the only safe thing in the world she could grasp.

27. What do the questions in paragraph 3 tell the reader about Brett's experience?
a. He was angry, confused, and resentful toward his mother's pregnancy and his little sister.
b. He was undecided about how he felt about his mother's pregnancy.
c. He was excited about the prospect of becoming a big brother for the first time.
d. He was both happy and upset about the prospect of becoming a big brother for the first time.

28. What impact do the statements by Brett's mother and father have on the reader's understanding of the essay?
a. They introduce doubt as to whether or not Brett's interpretation of these events is really accurate.
b. They add a humanizing element to this memory, as the reader can hear the voices of Brett's parents as they soothed their son.
c. They provide information that takes the story in an unexpected new direction.
d. They add a new perspective of the events that took place, which changes how the reader may interpret the memory.

29. What is the significance of Brett's mother whispering "I love you, baby" into his ear?
a. By calling Brett "baby," she is making fun of Brett.
b. By calling Brett "baby," she makes Brett think she doesn't care about what he is feeling.
c. By calling Brett "baby," she makes Brett feel like he is a baby instead of a big kid.
d. By calling Brett "baby," she reassures him that he is just as important to her as the new baby.

30. Which sentence could be deleted from paragraph 5 without changing the overall message of the paragraph?

    a. sentence 17
    b. sentence 19
    c. sentence 20
    d. sentence 21

31. Which of the following sentences from the essay most clearly explains why the birth of Brett's sister was his most memorable experience?

    a. I knew then that nothing would come between my parents and me.
    b. When we got to my mom's room, my dad came out and gave me the biggest hug I'd ever gotten.
    c. And I learned that I had enough love in me for a new member of our family, too.
    d. None of the above; Brett doesn't explain in his essay why the birth of his sister was his most memorable experience.

32. Which of the following sentences would be the best conclusion for this essay?

    a. The love that I felt in that moment overwhelmed me, making it an experience I will remember all of my life.
    b. There was nothing in the world that could have stopped me from becoming the best big brother I could be.
    c. My parents' love had given me the strength to make it through this moment, and I will be forever grateful for their support.
    d. Though I was willing to accept that I was no longer an only child, I also knew that from this moment on, nothing would ever really be the same.

The following address was given by President Franklin D. Roosevelt on Dec. 8, 1941, the day after Pearl Harbor was attacked by Japan.

    Mr. Vice President, Mr. Speaker, Members of the Senate, and of the House of Representatives:

    Yesterday, December 7th, 1941 -- a date which will live in infamy -- the United States of America was suddenly and deliberately attacked by naval and air forces of the Empire of Japan.

    The United States was at peace with that nation and, at the solicitation of Japan, was still in conversation with its government and its emperor looking toward the maintenance of peace in the Pacific.

    Indeed, one hour after Japanese air squadrons had commenced bombing in the American island of Oahu, the Japanese ambassador to the United States and his colleague delivered to our Secretary of State a formal reply to a recent American message. And while this reply stated that it seemed useless to continue the existing diplomatic negotiations, it contained no threat or hint of war or of armed attack.

    It will be recorded that the distance of Hawaii from Japan makes it obvious that the attack was deliberately planned many days or even weeks ago. During the intervening time, the Japanese government has deliberately sought to deceive the United States by false statements and expressions of hope for continued peace.

The attack yesterday on the Hawaiian islands has caused severe damage to American naval and military forces. I regret to tell you that very many American lives have been lost. In addition, American ships have been reported torpedoed on the high seas between San Francisco and Honolulu.

Yesterday, the Japanese government also launched an attack against Malaya.

Last night, Japanese forces attacked Hong Kong.

Last night, Japanese forces attacked Guam.

Last night, Japanese forces attacked the Philippine Islands.

Last night, the Japanese attacked Wake Island.

And this morning, the Japanese attacked Midway Island.

Japan has, therefore, undertaken a surprise offensive extending throughout the Pacific area. The facts of yesterday and today speak for themselves. The people of the United States have already formed their opinions and well understand the implications to the very life and safety of our nation.

As commander in chief of the Army and Navy, I have directed that all measures be taken for our defense. But always will our whole nation remember the character of the onslaught against us.

No matter how long it may take us to overcome this premeditated invasion, the American people in their righteous might will win through to absolute victory.

I believe that I interpret the will of the Congress and of the people when I assert that we will not only defend ourselves to the uttermost, but will make it very certain that this form of treachery shall never again endanger us.

Hostilities exist. There is no blinking at the fact that our people, our territory, and our interests are in grave danger.

With confidence in our armed forces, with the unbounding determination of our people, we will gain the inevitable triumph -- so help us God.

I ask that the Congress declare that since the unprovoked and dastardly attack by Japan on Sunday, December 7th, 1941, a state of war has existed between the United States and the Japanese empire.

33. Which of the following is a fact presented in this address?

a. No matter how long it may take us to overcome this premeditated invasion, the American people in their righteous might will win through to absolute victory.
b. But always will our whole nation remember the character of the onslaught against us.
c. I believe that I interpret the will of the Congress and of the people when I assert that we will not only defend ourselves to the uttermost, but will make it very certain that this form of treachery shall never again endanger us.
d. Last night, Japanese forces attacked Hong Kong.

34. Where might you look to find more information about the bombing of Pearl Harbor?

   a. an American history textbook
   b. home movies
   c. transcripts of interviews with the mayor of your town
   d. transcripts of interviews with the current president

35. Based on the information presented, you think that Congress should approve the president's request to declare war. What reasoning might you use to convince your class you are right?

   a. Roosevelt is the president, and his authority should not be questioned.
   b. Roosevelt's reasoning is heartfelt and it feels like the right thing to do, even if there are not enough facts presented.
   c. The president presents a compelling case supported by facts and logic that makes sense.
   d. Roosevelt is clearly considering the consequences such a decision would have on his political party.

Use the following image to answer questions 36 – 40.

36. What is most likely happening in the picture?

   a. People have gathered at a cemetery for some kind of memorial service.
   b. A little boy is visiting the grave of a loved one.
   c. A celebration for a national holiday is being held.
   d. There is no way to tell what is happening in the picture.

37. How would you describe the mood of the scene?

   a. jovial and celebratory
   b. solemn and reverent
   c. bright and airy
   d. severe and admonitory

38. You learn that one of the names on the plaque belongs to the little boy's father. How does this new information alter your interpretation of the picture?

    a. It changes the original interpretation from a neutral one to a negative one.

    b. It makes it clearer why the people in the background are there.

    c. It makes it easier to understand the reason for the memorial.

    d. It provides a deeper understanding of what the boy is doing and feeling.

39. Which of the following questions might you pose to a group of your classmates to start a critical discussion about the details of the image?

    a. What event does this memorial commemorate, and why do you think so?

    b. Where was the picture taken?

    c. Who is the photographer, and what was his or her assignment?

    d. Was this picture ever published?

40. What is the likely purpose of the photo?

    a. to show the ideology behind a historic event

    b. to make a political statement about a recent event

    c. to show the lasting impact of a tragic event

    d. to inform the public about a recent event

41. What is the grammatical error in the following sentence?

    Aware that his decision would affect the rest of his life, the college Ben chose was Harvard.

    a. The subject and the verb do not agree.

    b. The sentence contains a comma splice.

    c. There is a dangling modifier.

    d. There is no error.

42. Which word in the following sentence is an adverb?

    The present was wrapped expertly by a professional at the store.

    a. present

    b. wrapped

    c. expertly

    d. professional

43. What does the underlined word in the following sentence mean?

    The students' excitement about the beginning of summer vacation <u>pervaded</u> the whole classroom.

    a. stood at attention

    b. spread throughout

    c. explained

    d. took note

44. The phrase "going into the fold" refers to

    a. joining or rejoining a group.

    b. rejecting an idea.

    c. holding true to a belief.

    d. starting a new journey.

45. hyperventilation : air :: hyperthermia :

    a. hair

    b. air

    c. heat

    d. money

46. Which of the following would best explain a speaker's feelings?

    a. I appreciated the view.

    b. I had an issue with the clerk's tone.

    c. Artie yelled at me.

    d. Kelly's gift of flowers warmed my heart.

47. Which sentence is punctuated correctly?

    a. We were uncertain about the terrain ahead; and had lost the map.

    b. These were the items on the shopping list: eggs, milk, bread, peanut butter, and jelly.

    c. Is there any way that we can meet later.

    d. Mary had an appointment at 3 p.m.; George had one at 4 p.m.

48. Which of the following answer choices is spelled correctly?

    a. intrude

    b. aclimate

    c. wisen

    d. alude

49. Which of the following is an example of a compound sentence?

    a. I sat outside the room.

    b. Anton needed to get to school, but he first had to stop at the store and pick up some napkins.

    c. Laura reminded her husband that the rent was due, and she looked up their checking account balance online.

    d. Because there was no time to plan for a party, we decided to cancel my birthday celebrations.

50. Where would you look if you needed to find another word for "pardon"?

    a. a dictionary

    b. a thesaurus

    c. an index

    d. a glossary

Mathematics

In order to receive a high school diploma in a few years, you will need to be proficient in math. Schools stress math because it's very important, in many different areas of life. At times, it may seem as if what you're learning won't be very useful in everyday life, but that isn't the case. Math is very useful, in many different ways. Besides being useful, math is also fascinating, and you can get a lot of enjoyment out of solving difficult problems on your own. These practice questions can help you improve your math skills.

1. Which of the following is listed in order from *greatest to least*?

    a. $2\frac{1}{4}, \frac{32}{5}, \frac{4}{5}, -5, -2$

    b. $\frac{32}{5}, 2\frac{1}{4}, \frac{4}{5}, -2, -5$

    c. $-5, -2, \frac{32}{5}, \frac{4}{5}, 2\frac{1}{4}$

    d. $\frac{32}{5}, 2\frac{1}{4}, \frac{4}{5}, -5, -2$

2. Ana has completed approximately $\frac{2}{7}$ of her research paper. Which of the following best represents the percentage of the paper she has completed?

    a. 24%

    b. 26%

    c. 27%

    d. 29%

3. What is the square root of the area represented in the model below?

    a. 3

    b. 12

    c. 4

    d. 16

4. A mathematics test has a 4:2 ratio of data analysis problems to algebra problems. If the test has 18 algebra problems, how many data analysis problems are on the test?

    a. 24

    b. 36

    c. 38

    d. 28

5. Elijah has prepared $2\frac{1}{2}$ gallons of lemonade to distribute to guests at a party. If there are 25 guests, how much lemonade is available to each guest, given that each guest receives an equal amount?

    a. $\frac{1}{8}$ of a gallon

    b. $\frac{1}{6}$ of a gallon

    c. $\frac{1}{12}$ of a gallon

    d. $\frac{1}{10}$ of a gallon

6. How many one-fourths are contained in $8\frac{1}{2}$?

    a.   34

    b.   64

    c.   36

    d.   17

7. Which number sentence is represented by the model shown below?

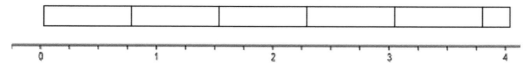

    a. $4 \div \frac{3}{4} = 5\frac{1}{3}$

    b. $4 \div \frac{2}{3} = 5\frac{1}{3}$

    c. $4 \div \frac{3}{4} = 5\frac{1}{4}$

    d. $4 \div \frac{2}{3} = 5\frac{1}{4}$

8. Which number sentence is represented by the number line below?

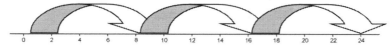

    a. $24 \div 2 = 12$

    b. $8 + 16 = 24$

    c. $8 \times 2 = 16$

    d. $24 \div 3 = 8$

9. Edward drove 840 miles at a speed of 60 miles per hour. How many hours did he travel?

    a.   14

    b.   16

    c.   17

    d.   18

10. A bag of coffee costs $9.85 and contains 16 ounces of coffee. Which of the following best represents the cost per ounce?

    a. $0.67
    b. $0.64
    c. $0.65
    d. $0.62

11. Which of the following is equivalent to $4^3 + 12 \div 4 + 8^2 \times 3$?

    a. 249
    b. 393
    c. 211
    d. 259

12. Amy deposits $1 in her savings account during Month 1. For each subsequent month, she deposits an amount equal to the square of the number of the month. Douglas deposits the same amount in his savings account During Month 1. However, for each subsequent month, he deposits twice the amount deposited the previous month. Which is the first month that the amount deposited by Douglas exceeds the amount deposited by Amy?

    a. Month 4
    b. Month 6
    c. Month 7
    d. Month 8

13. Hannah will donate a total of $1,400 in equal amounts to 13 charities. Which of the following is a reasonable estimate for the amount donated to each charity?

    a. More than $110 but less than $115
    b. More than $105 but less than $110
    c. More than $120 but less than $125
    d. More than $115 but less than $120

14. The original price of a jacket is $36.95. The jacket is discounted by 25%. Before tax, which of the following best represents the cost of the jacket?

    a. $27.34
    b. $27.71
    c. $28.82
    d. $29.56

15. A car dealership is having a blowout sale. Douglas finds a car sale-priced at $36,549.15. The car was originally priced at $42,999. What percentage discount would Douglas receive?

    a. 12%
    b. 15%
    c. 18%
    d. 20%

16. A bottle of lotion contains 20 fluid ounces and costs $3.96. Which of the following best represents the cost per fluid ounce?

    a. $0.18
    b. $0.20
    c. $0.22
    d. $0.24

17. What is the 18ᵗʰ term in the sequence$-7, -14, -21, -28, ...$?

    a. −133
    b. −126
    c. −119
    d. −112

18. Triangle A has side lengths of 12 cm, 8 cm, and 16 cm. Triangle B is related to Triangle A by a scale factor of $\frac{1}{4}$. Which of the following represents the dimensions of Triangle B?

    a. 4 cm, 2 cm, 8 cm
    b. 2 cm, 3 cm, 8 cm
    c. 3 cm, 2 cm, 4 cm
    d. 6 cm, 4 cm, 8 cm

19. A book has a width of 2.5 decimeters. What is the width of the book in centimeters?

    a. 0.25 centimeters
    b. 25 centimeters
    c. 250 centimeters
    d. 0.025 centimeters

20. The approximate volumes of spheres with different radii are listed in the table below.

Radius	Volume
2	33.49 in³
4	267.95 in³
6	904.32 in³
8	2,143.57 in³

If the volume of each sphere is equal to some ratio multiplied by the product of the cubed radius and pi (π), what is the ratio?

    a. 4
    b. $\frac{1}{3}$
    c. 3
    d. $\frac{4}{3}$

21. Which of the following graphs accurately portrays the relationship between number of feet and number of yards?

a.

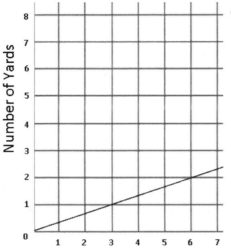

c.

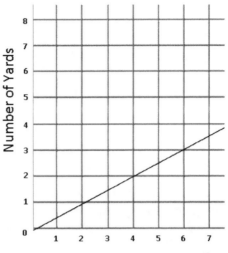

b.

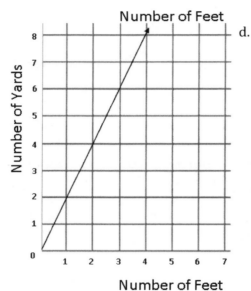

d.

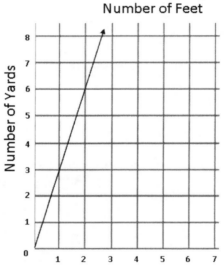

22. Given the sequence represented in the table below, where *n* represents the position of the term and a_n represents the value of the term, which of the following describes the relationship between the position number and the value of the term?

n	1	2	3	4	5	6
a_n	5	2	−1	−4	−7	−10

    a.   Multiply *n* by 2 and subtract 4
    b.   Multiply *n* by 2 and subtract 3
    c.   Multiply *n* by −3 and add 8
    d.   Multiply *n* by −4 and add 1

23. The number 123 is the 11th term in a sequence with a constant rate of change. Which of the following sequences has this number as its 11th term?
    a. 5, 17, 29, 41, ...
    b. 3, 15, 27, 39, ...
    c. −1, 11, 23, 35, ...
    d. 1, 13, 25, 37, ...

24. Given the equation represented by the algebra tiles shown below, where  represents x and ▢ represents the positive integer 1, which of the following represents the solution?

    a. $x = 6$
    b. $x = 9$
    c. $x = 3$
    d. $x = 12$

25. Kevin pays $12.95 for a text messaging service plus $0.07 for each text message he sends. Which of the following equations could be used to represent the total cost, y, when x represents the number of text messages sent?
    a. $y = \$12.95x + \$0.07$
    b. $y = \$13.02x$
    c. $y = \dfrac{\$12.95}{\$0.07}x$
    d. $y = \$0.07x + \$12.95$

26. Hannah draws two supplementary angles. One angle measures 34°. What is the measure of the other angle?
    a. 56°
    b. 66°
    c. 146°
    d. 326°

27. The cost for different numbers of boxes of doughnuts is shown in the table below:

Number of Boxes (b)	Total Cost (c)
4	$15.00
7	$26.25
12	$45.00
18	$67.50

Which equation can be used to find the cost per box, x? Let c represent the total cost and b represent the number of boxes.

 a. $x = bc$
 b. $x = \dfrac{b}{c}$
 c. $x = \dfrac{c}{b}$
 d. $x = c + b$

28. A triangle has the following angle measures: 98°, 47°, and 35°. What type of triangle is it?

 a. Obtuse
 b. Right
 c. Acute
 d. Equiangular

29. Which figure has 5 faces and 8 edges?

 a. Triangular pyramid
 b. Cube
 c. Square pyramid
 d. Triangular prism

30. Which figure has two circular bases and a lateral face?

 a. Cone
 b. Prism
 c. Cylinder
 d. Sphere

31. What ordered pair is shown on the graph below?

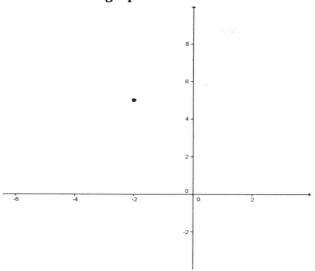

   a. $(-2, 5)$
   b. $(-2, -5)$
   c. $(2, 5)$
   d. $(2, -5)$

32. Edward draws a triangle with vertices at $(1, 4)$, $(5, 1)$, and $(5, 6)$. If he wishes to reflect the triangle across the x-axis, which of the following vertices should he plot?

   a. $(-1, 4), (-5, 1), (-5, 6)$
   b. $(1, -4), (5, -1), (5, -6)$
   c. $(-1, -4), (-5, -1), (-5, -6)$
   d. $(4, 1), (1, 5), (6, 5)$

33. A carpenter must fix a broken section of a kitchen cabinet. The intact portion of the cabinet forms a 76 degree angle with the wall. The width of the cabinet is supposed to form a 90 degree angle with the wall. What angle measure should the carpenter use when cutting the piece that will fit next to the 76 degree angle?

   a. $12°$
   b. $14°$
   c. $104°$
   d. $136°$

34. Which of the following represents the net of a triangular prism?

a.

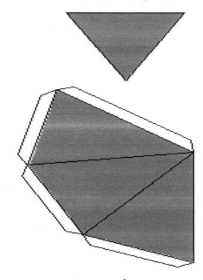

c.

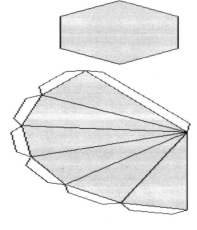

b.

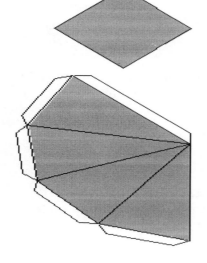

d.

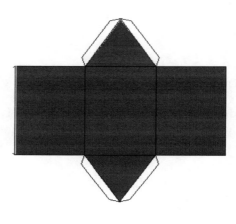

35. A circle has a radius of 23 cm. Which of the following is the best estimate for the circumference of the circle?

a. 71.76 cm
b. 143.52 cm
c. 144.44 cm
d. 72.22 cm

36. Which three-dimensional figure is approximated by the net shown below?

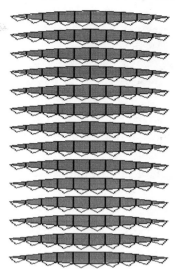

    a.   Cone
    b.   Rectangular prism
    c.   Sphere
    d.   Cylinder

37. Triangle ABC has side lengths of 18 cm, 14 cm, and 12 cm. Which of the following dimensions belong to a similar triangle?

    a.   9 cm, 7 cm, 6 cm
    b.   36 cm, 28 cm, 22 cm
    c.   6 cm, 7 cm, 4 cm
    d.   27 cm, 21 cm, 15 cm

38. Given the triangle below, which of the following is the best estimate for the perimeter of the triangle?

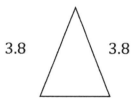

3.8   3.8

4.2 in

    a.   10 in
    b.   11 in
    c.   12 in
    d.   13 in

39. In the formula for the volume of the figure shown below, written as $V = B \cdot h$, h represents the height of the prism when it rests one of its bases. What does the B represent?

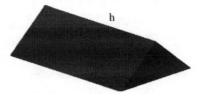

a. $\frac{1}{3}bh$, where b represents the length of the triangle's base and h represents the triangle's height.

b. bh, where b represents the length of the triangle's base and h represents the triangle's height.

c. $2bh$, where b represents the length of triangle's base and h represents the triangle's height.

d. $\frac{1}{2}bh$, where b represents the length of triangle's base and h represents the triangle's height.

40. A rectangular prism has a length of 14.3 cm, a width of 8.9 cm, and a height of 11.7 cm. Which of the following is the best estimate for the volume of the rectangular prism?

a. $1,512 \text{ cm}^3$
b. $1,287 \text{ cm}^3$
c. $1,386 \text{ cm}^3$
d. $1,620 \text{ cm}^3$

41. A can has a radius of 3.5 cm and a height of 8 cm. Which of the following best represents the volume of the can?

a. 294.86 cm^3
b. 298.48 cm^3
c. 307.72 cm^3
d. 309.24 cm^3

42. Fred designs a candy box in the shape of a triangular prism. The base of each triangular face measures 4 inches, while the height of the prism is 7 inches. Given that the length of the prism is 11 inches, what is the volume of the candy box?

a. 102 in^3
b. 128 in^3
c. 154 in^3
d. 308 in^3

43. Miranda rolls a standard die and spins a spinner with 4 equal sections. Which of the following represents the sample space?

a. 10
b. 12
c. 24
d. 36

44. What is the sample space when flipping three coins?

   a. 6
   b. 8
   c. 12
   d. 15

45. A hat contains 6 red die, 4 green die, and 2 blue die. What is the probability that Sarah pulls out a blue die, replaces it, and then pulls out a green die?

   a. $\frac{1}{18}$
   b. $\frac{1}{3}$
   c. $\frac{1}{2}$
   d. $\frac{1}{16}$

46. Eli wishes to compare the changes in monthly deposits made to his savings account over a period of two years. Which of the following is the best graphical tool for analyzing the data?

   a. Line graph
   b. Histogram
   c. Line plot
   d. Bar graph

47. The histogram below represents the overall GRE scores for a sample of college students. Which of the following is a true statement?

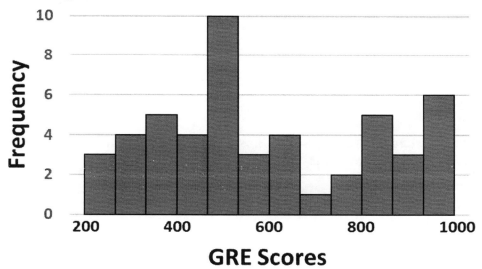

   a. The range of GRE scores is approximately 600.
   b. The average GRE score is 750.
   c. The median GRE score is approximately 500.
   d. The fewest number of college students had an approximate score of 800.

48. The ages at which a sample of female dogs is spayed is shown below. Based on this sample, what is the average age a female dog gets spayed? 6, 7, 2, 8, 4, 1, 7, 8, 3, 1, 8, 2

    a. 3.75
    b. 4
    c. 4.75
    d. 5

49. Student scores on Mrs. Thompson's last math test are shown below. Which of the following is the best representation of class performance?

      76, 39, 87, 85, 91, 93, 86, 90, 77, 89, 74, 82, 68, 86, 79

    a. Mean
    b. Median
    c. Mode
    d. Range

50. Amy rolled a die and flipped a coin. What is the probability that she rolled an even number and got heads?

    a. $\frac{1}{4}$
    b. $\frac{1}{2}$
    c. $\frac{3}{4}$
    d. $\frac{1}{3}$

51. Which of the following is listed in order from *least to greatest*?

    a. $-2\frac{3}{4}, -2\frac{7}{8}, -\frac{1}{5}, \frac{2}{5}, \frac{1}{8}$
    b. $-\frac{1}{5}, \frac{1}{8}, \frac{2}{5}, -2\frac{3}{4}, -2\frac{7}{8}$
    c. $-2\frac{7}{8}, -2\frac{3}{4}, -\frac{1}{5}, \frac{1}{8}, \frac{2}{5}$
    d. $\frac{1}{8}, \frac{2}{5}, -\frac{1}{5}, -2\frac{7}{8}, -2\frac{3}{4}$

52. Amanda has finished 80% of a grant proposal. Which of the following fractions represents the amount she has finished?

    a. $\frac{3}{4}$
    b. $\frac{7}{9}$
    c. $\frac{4}{5}$
    d. $\frac{6}{7}$

53. In a square built with unit squares, which of the following would represent the square root of the square?

    a. The number of unit squares comprising a side
    b. The total number of unit squares within the square
    c. Half of the total number of unit squares within the square
    d. The number of unit squares comprising the perimeter of the square

54. According to the order of operations, which of the following steps should be completed immediately following the evaluation of the squared number when evaluating the expression $9 - 18^2 \times 2 + 12 \div 4$?

    a. Subtract 18^2 from 9
    b. Multiply the squared value by 2
    c. Divide 12 by 4
    d. Add 2 and 12

55. A publishing company has been given 29 manuscripts to review. If the company divides the work equally amongst 8 editors, which of the following represents the number of manuscript each editor will review?

    a. $3\frac{3}{5}$
    b. $3\frac{5}{8}$
    c. $3\frac{7}{9}$
    d. $3\frac{2}{3}$

56. Given the counters shown below, where ⬤ represents negative 1 and ⚪ represents positive 1, what is the sum?

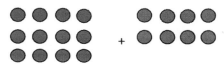

    a. −20
    b. 4
    c. 20
    d. −4

57. A parcel of land has 35 mature trees for every 3 acres. How many mature trees can be found on 18 of the acres?

    a. 206
    b. 212
    c. 210
    d. 214

58. Which of the following is equivalent to $-8^2 + (17 - 9) \times 4 + 7$?

    a. −217
    b. 24
    c. −64
    d. −25

59. Jason chooses a number that is the square root of four less than two times Amy's number. If Amy's number is 20, what is Jason's number?

    a. 6
    b. 7
    c. 8
    d. 9

60. Gitta brings $2,082 on a business trip. The trip will last 7 days. Which of the following is the best estimate for the amount of money she has to spend per day?

    a. $200
    b. $320
    c. $240
    d. $300

61. Josiah walks $8\frac{3}{5}$ miles on Monday. Which of the following is equivalent to the number of miles he walked?

    a. 8.8
    b. 8.6
    c. 8.7
    d. 8.4

62. Brianna used five $\frac{3}{4}$ cups of sugar while baking. How many cups of sugar did she use in all?

    a. $3\frac{2}{3}$
    b. $3\frac{3}{4}$
    c. $3\frac{1}{4}$
    d. $3\frac{1}{2}$

63. Robert secures three new clients every eight months. After how many months has he secured 24 new clients?

    a. 64
    b. 58
    c. 52
    d. 66

64. A landscaping company charges $25 per $\frac{1}{2}$-acre to mow a yard. The company is offering a 20% discount for the month of May. If Douglas has a two-acre yard, how much will the company charge?

    a. $65
    b. $80
    c. $70
    d. $75

65. A house is priced at $278,000. The price of the house has been reduced by $12,600. Which of the following best represents the percentage of the reduction?

    a. 3%
    b. 4%
    c. 5%
    d. 6%

66. A 20-ounce drink costs $1.19. Which of the following best represents the cost per ounce?
a. $0.07
b. $0.06
c. $0.04
d. $0.08

67. Mel studied 25 hours per week when he took four college courses. If he spends the same amount of time studying per course, how many hours will he spend studying when he takes five college courses?
a. 30.75
b. 32.50
c. 31.75
d. 31.25

68. A cone has a radius of 4 cm and an approximate volume of 150.72 cm³. What is the height of the cone?
a. 7 cm
b. 9 cm
c. 8 cm
d. 12 cm

69. Which of the following graphs represents the relationship between the side length of a square and its perimeter?

a.

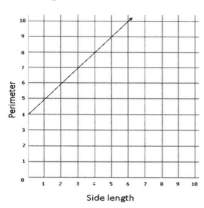

c.

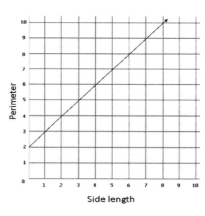

b.

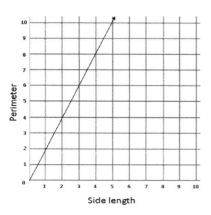

d.

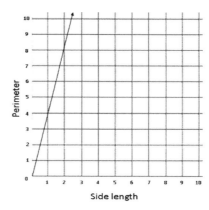

70. Which of the following represents the relationship between the diameter of a circle and its circumference?

a.

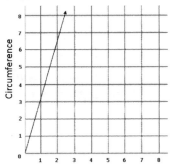

c.

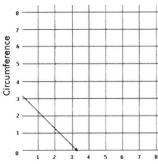

b.

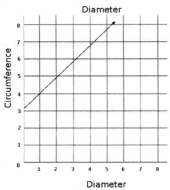

d.

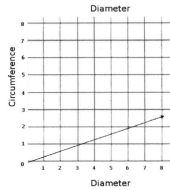

Science

Science topics are both informative and fascinating. Learning about the amazing diversity of life forms on the planet is one of the most enjoyable parts of school for many students, and for some, biology becomes a life-long pursuit. The same is true about the study of our planet, our solar system, and the universe. Other areas of science are equally as engrossing. There are many difference facets of science, and all of them have an impact on our lives in a myriad of ways. You'll need to do well in this subject in order to earn your high school diploma. Here are some questions that can help you make sure you're on track when it comes to science.

1. A botanist examining a collection of related plants of a certain species notices that plants with white flowers tend to be taller than plants with yellow flowers. Which of the following is the most likely explanation for this?

    a. White flowers and tallness are both dominant traits.
    b. White flowers and tallness are both recessive traits.
    c. The genes for white flowers and tallness are on the same chromosome.
    d. The genes for white flowers and tallness are on different chromosomes.

2. Which of the following organisms is likely to have the largest number of cells?

    a. A housefly
    b. A bacterium
    c. A field mouse
    d. A mature pine tree

3. "For every action there is an equal and opposite reaction." What is this statement?

    a. Newton's First Law
    b. Newton's Second Law
    c. Newton's Third Law
    d. The First Law of Thermodynamics

4. Which of the following is NOT considered a renewable energy source?

    a. Hydroelectricity
    b. Natural gas
    c. Solar energy
    d. Wind energy

Directions: Use the information below and your knowledge of science to answer questions 5–6.

Twenty specimens of a new species of butterfly are introduced to a small forest. The following is a graph of the number of butterflies of this species in the forest as a function of time.

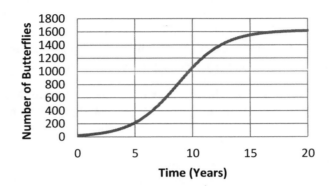

5. According to this graph, about how many butterflies were in the forest five years after they were first introduced?

    a. 200
    b. 400
    c. 1,000
    d. The graph does not give this information.

6. Which of the following best describes the growth of the butterfly population after a long period of time, as shown by this graph?

    a. The butterflies will eventually die out because they will stop reproducing.
    b. The butterflies will keep increasing without limit because new mutations will keep increasing their variety.
    c. The butterflies will eventually tend toward a stable number because there is a limit to how many butterflies the available resources will support.
    d. The butterflies will eventually tend toward a stable number because they are genetically preprogrammed to reach a particular population size.

7. Francis finds that he is able to dissolve six times as much sugar in a glass of water as he can dissolve salt in the same amount of water. Which of the following can he accurately conclude from this?

    a. The solubility of sugar in water is higher than the solubility of salt in water.
    b. The solubility of salt in water is higher than the solubility of sugar in water.
    c. The solubility of water in sugar is higher than the solubility of water in salt.
    d. The solubility of water in salt is higher than the solubility of water in sugar.

8. If Francis used twice as much water, would he get a different result for the solubility of the salt?

    a. Yes, because the more water he uses, the more salt he can dissolve in it.
    b. Yes, because the more water he uses, the less salt he can dissolve in it.
    c. No, because solubility is a property of a material; it doesn't depend on the amount.
    d. No, because it would only have changed his measurement for the sugar, not for the salt.

9. What are comets mostly made of?

   a. Ice
   b. Iron
   c. Plasma
   d. Nothing; comets are optical illusions with no physical substance.

10. A comet called 12P/Pons-Brooks last passed by the Earth in 1954. The time before that, it passed by the Earth in 1884. In what year is it likely to pass by the Earth again?

   a. 2024
   b. 2084
   c. 2134
   d. If it has already passed by the Earth twice, this comet will never pass by the Earth again.

11. What structures inside the cell are primarily responsible for generating energy for the cell?

   a. Cytoplasm
   b. Mitochondria
   c. Nuclei
   d. Ribosomes

12. Which of the following best describes why an ice cube left on the counter at room temperature will warm up and melt?

   a. The ice cube will radiate cold into its surroundings.
   b. Cold will be conducted from the ice cube into the counter and air.
   c. The counter will radiate heat into the ice cube.
   d. Heat will be conducted from the counter and air into the ice cube.

13. How will the mass of the ice cube compare to the mass of the puddle of water left after it melts? (Assume that no water evaporates while the ice is melting.)

   a. The water will have a larger mass because water is denser than ice.
   b. The ice will have a larger mass because ice is denser than water.
   c. The ice will have a larger mass because solids have more mass than liquids.
   d. The ice and the water will have the same mass because mass is conserved.

Directions: Use the information below and your knowledge of science to answer questions 14–17.

A student measures the average temperature where he lives in each of four different months during three consecutive years.

Year	January	April	July	October
2011	73°F	68°F	53°F	63°F
2012	75°F	65°F	54°F	66°F
2013	71°F	65°F	58°F	63°F

14. What is the three-year average temperature in July where the student lives?

   a. 54°F
   b. 55°F
   c. 56°F
   d. 57°F

15. How would the student's results have changed had he taken the measurements in degrees Celsius instead of Fahrenheit?

 a. The measurements would have been less accurate.
 b. The measurements would have been more accurate.
 c. The numbers would be different, but they would have been just as useful.
 d. There would be no change; the numbers would be exactly the same.

16. From these data, where is the student likely to be located?

 a. On the equator because the temperature never goes below freezing
 b. Near the ocean because there is a large variation in temperature
 c. The Northern Hemisphere, because the temperature is about the same in spring (April) and fall (October)
 d. The Southern Hemisphere, because it is hottest in January and coldest in July

17. What instrument is the student likely to have used to take these measurements?

 a. An anemometer
 b. A barometer
 c. A multimeter
 d. A thermometer

18. Which of these organs is NOT part of the respiratory system?

 a. Heart
 b. Lungs
 c. Trachea
 d. Diaphragm

19. Which system of the human body is responsible for gathering and processing information?

 a. Circulatory system
 b. Digestive system
 c. Nervous system
 d. Reproductive system

Directions: Use the information below and your knowledge of science to answer questions 20–22.

A student measures the length of a hanging spring when different masses are attached to the free end. (He takes the measurements when the mass is hanging motionless, not bouncing up and down.) He records the following data:

Mass:	Length:
0 g	30.0 cm
100 g	33.1 cm
200 g	36.3 cm
300 g	39.2 cm
400 g	42.5 cm

20. Which of the following best explains what is causing the length of the spring to change?

    a.   The pull of gravity on the mass exerts a downward force that stretches the spring.

    b.   The mass exerts a gravitational force directly on the spring, causing it to stretch.

    c.   The pull of gravity on the spring is cancelled by the mass, causing it to compress.

    d.   The spring exerts a gravitational force on the mass, pulling it upward and compressing the spring.

21. In what direction is the net force on the mass when the student takes his measurements?

    a.   The direction on the net force is upward.

    b.   The direction on the net force is downward.

    c.   The direction on the net force is zero.

    d.   The direction on the net force cannot be determined.

22. In the table, what does the *g* stand for after the mass measurements?

    a.   Gauge

    b.   Grams

    c.   Gravity

    d.   Ground

23. A lunar eclipse always happens during which phase of the moon?

    a.   New moon

    b.   Full moon

    c.   Crescent moon

    d.   Gibbous moon

24. Which gas makes up the majority of the atmosphere?

    a.   Carbon dioxide

    b.   Nitrogen

    c.   Oxygen

    d.   Water vapor

25. The marks on the following map (from the U.S. Geological Survey Web site) show the locations of volcanoes. What is the best explanation for the fact that many of the volcanoes seem to be clustered along certain lines?

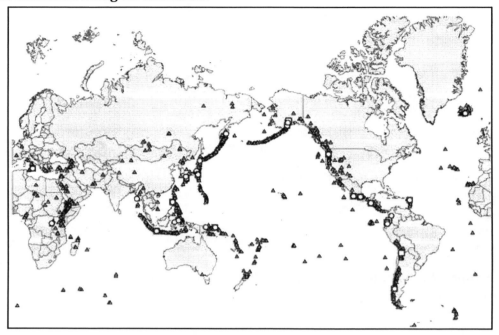

a. Volcanoes tend to form along the edges of continental plates.
b. Volcanoes tend to form along the Earth's magnetic field lines.
c. Volcanoes tend to form near warm ocean currents.
d. Volcanoes tend to spread; when one forms it, gives rise to other volcanoes near it.

26. Anemia is a disorder of the blood in which insufficient oxygen reaches the organs. A deficiency in which component of the blood is likely to cause anemia?

a. Red blood cells
b. White blood cells
c. Plasma
d. Platelets

27. Sea urchins belong to which animal phylum?

a. Arthropoda (arthropods)
b. Chordata (chordates)
c. Echinodermata (echinoderms)
d. Mollusca (molluscs)

64

28. What kind of cell is pictured below?

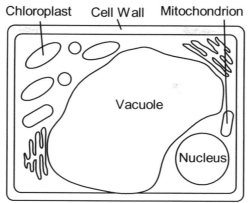

a. Animal cell
b. Bacterium
c. Paramecium
d. Plant cell

29. Suppose you have two blocks of cement and two blocks of polished marble. Between which combination of blocks would you expect the friction to be greatest?

a. Between the two cement blocks
b. Between the two marble blocks
c. Between one block of cement and one block of marble
d. Between any two blocks

30. What happens when the buoyant force on a submerged object is greater than the force of gravity on the object?

a. The object sinks.
b. The object floats.
c. The object neither sinks nor floats but hangs suspended in the same position.
d. This can't happen; the buoyant force is always less than or equal to the force of gravity.

31. In what units is electrical current measured?

a. Amperes
b. Joules
c. Ohms
d. Volts

Directions: Use the information below and your knowledge of science to answer questions 32–33.

During a lightning storm, a student counts three seconds between seeing the flash of lightning and hearing the report.

32. In order to know how far away the lightning was, what else would the student need to know?

a. The air temperature
b. The height of the storm clouds
c. The time of day
d. The speed of sound

33. What would it mean if the student heard the report first before seeing the lightning bolt?

    a. The storm is moving away.
    b. The lightning bolt is less than a mile away.
    c. The air pressure is very low, which means there might be danger of a cyclone.
    d. This can't happen; you always see the lightning before you hear it.

34. The corpse flower is a Sumatran flower that smells like rotting meat. Which of the following is the most likely reason it would have developed such a scent?

    a. To attract mates
    b. To drive away predators
    c. To attract flies to pollinate it
    d. To inhibit the growth of other plants nearby

35. Which of the following accurately describes a difference between sound waves and light waves?

    a. Light waves have a period and amplitude; sound waves do not.
    b. Unlike light waves, sound waves require a medium to travel through.
    c. Unlike sound waves, all light waves have the same frequency.
    d. Light waves can be reflected or refracted; sound waves cannot.

36. Which of the following types of electromagnetic wave has the largest wavelength?

    a. Infrared light
    b. Ultraviolet light
    c. Visible light
    d. Radio waves

37. What is the main source of energy in a star?

    a. Nuclear fission of helium into hydrogen
    b. Nuclear fusion of hydrogen into helium
    c. Chemical reactions between the various gases in the star
    d. Electricity generated by the friction between the gases

38. Past the edge of the continental shelf, the ocean floor drops in the continental slope and then flattens out again in a deep underwater plain. What is this part of the ocean floor called?

    a. Abyssal plain
    b. Mid-ocean ridge
    c. Subcontinental plain
    d. Oceanic trench

Directions: Use the information below and your knowledge of science to answer questions 39–41.

Using a microscope, a student looks at a cross-section of a plant root and counts the number of cells she sees in each phase of mitosis. She gets the following results:

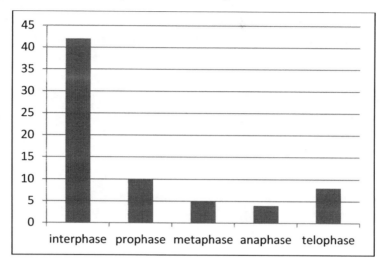

39. Which phase does each cell seem to spend the most time in?
    a. Interphase, because that is the phase in which she saw the most cells
    b. Anaphase, because that is the phase in which she saw the least cells
    c. Telophase, because that is the last phase she looked at
    d. Metaphase, because that is the phase directly in the middle

40. In which phase are all the chromosomes lined up in a plane?
    a. Prophase
    b. Metaphase
    c. Anaphase
    d. Telophase

41. How would this experiment have gone differently had the student looked at bacterial cells instead of plant root cells?
    a. The process would have worked just as well with bacterial cells.
    b. In bacterial cells, all the phases take exactly the same amount of time.
    c. She would not have been able to do the experiment with bacterial cells because they are too small to see, even with a microscope.
    d. The experiment would not have gone the same with bacterial cells because they do not undergo mitosis and do not have the same stages.

Social Studies

Imparting an understanding of humans and the societies and cultures they have created is the goal of social studies classes. This wide ranging field encompasses psychology, religion, economics, politics, anthropology, sociology, law, government, history, geography, and many other topics. No education is complete without a well-rounded course of studies in these areas. You'll find the following questions helpful as you seek to gain deeper insights into the world around you.

Civics/Government

1. The word 'suffrage' refers to what right?
- a. The right to vote in political elections
- b. The right to bear arms
- c. Protection from cruel and unusual punishment
- d. Protection from unreasonable search and seizures

2. There is a five-step process by which a bill becomes a law: introduction, committee action, floor action, final approval, and...
- a. Actualization.
- b. Authorization.
- c. Mandate.
- d. Enactment.

3. What purpose does the Necessary and Proper, or Elastic, Clause serve?
- a. It dictates the etiquette that must be observed on Capitol Hill.
- b. It is the final form of the annual budget.
- c. It grants Congress the power to pass legislation needed for the exercise of its explicit powers.
- d. None of the above

4. By what means can the Constitution be altered?
- a. An amendment
- b. A Supreme Court ruling
- c. A congressional vote
- d. A presidential veto

5. What is meant by the term "due process"?
- a. The government must administer justice in a way that protects its citizens from an intrusion on their rights.
- b. Criminal cases must be based in the wealth and status of the accused.
- c. Due process refers to the order in which congressional hearings take place.
- d. Due process refers to the series of trials a judge must preside over before being considered for the Supreme Court.

6. George Washington set a precedent for presidential term limits by leaving office after two. Washington's precedent was officially codified into law after which four-term President?
- a. Harry S. Truman
- b. Calvin Coolidge
- c. Theodore Roosevelt
- d. Franklin D. Roosevelt

7. Which of the following titles is used for the presiding officer of the House of Representatives?

a. Majority Leader
b. Speaker of the House
c. Majority Whip
d. President pro tempore

8. What is the name of Abraham Lincoln's executive order that freed all slaves in the Confederate states?

a. Abolition Proclamation
b. Writ of Habeas Corpus
c. Emancipation Proclamation
d. Magna Carta

9. In what type of election would a caucus be used?

a. Presidential election
b. Primary election
c. General election
d. Local election

10. Which of the following best describes the Electoral College?

a. The alma mater of the president
b. A body of people, representing the voters of each state, who cast formal votes to elect the members of the Supreme Court.
c. A body of people, representing the members of congress, who cast formal votes to elect the president and vice president.
d. The site at which members of the Supreme Court cast their votes.

11. Which of the following best describes the idea of popular sovereignty?

a. The government derives its power from the people.
b. The Supreme Court changes rulings depending on the attitudes of the people.
c. Leaders are well loved because they are in a position of authority.
d. The more populous states preside over less populated.

Geography

1. Geography is studied through which of the following main concepts?

a. Soil samples, rock structures, and climate patterns
b. Location, place, interaction between humans and their environment, movement and region
c. Regional language, culture, ethics, morals, and historical governments
d. Livestock, agriculture, sources of water, and wind patterns

2. When one refers to the Middle East, what are they referring to specifically?

a. A continent
b. A region
c. A country
d. A city

Use this map to answer questions 3 – 4:

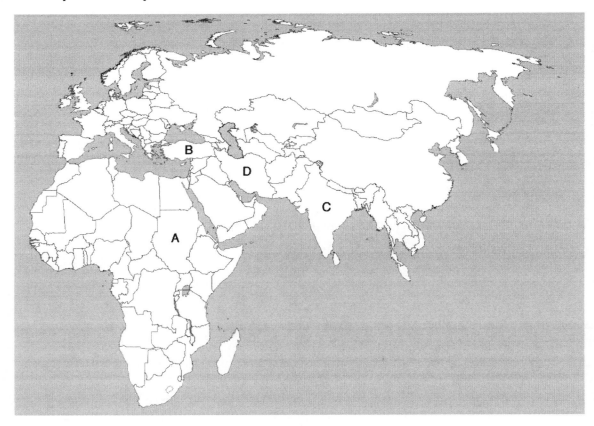

3. Which of the following nations share a border with Egypt?

   a. Israel
   b. Turkey
   c. India
   d. Iran

4. Which of the following nations would Egypt culturally relate to most closely?

   a. Israel
   b. Turkey
   c. India
   d. Iran

5. Civilizations located on fertile soil tend to cultivate and farm, while civilizations close to bodies of waters learn to fish. This is an example of what?

   a. Adaptation
   b. Cultural stereotypes
   c. Environmental limitations
   d. Geographic insulation

6. Which of the following is NOT a means of cultural diffusion?

a. The Internet
b. European colonialism
c. Immigration
d. Isolationism

7. What is the main cause of the desertification affecting the Sahara region of Africa?

a. Lack of farming
b. Deforestation
c. Heat
d. Drought

8. Which of the following best describes the gradual process of destruction or diminution by wind, water, or other natural means?

a. Flooding
b. Demolition
c. Erosion
d. Tectonic shift

9. What type of map is best suited for depicting battles and military campaigns?

a. Political map
b. Historical map
c. Physical map
d. None of the above

10. What map feature explains the colors, lines, and other symbols on a map?

a. Projection
b. Compass rose
c. Legend
d. Scale

History

1. Many explorers travelled the regions of the Louisiana Purchase. Which of these men's expeditions included the Arkansas River, the Rocky Mountains, and the Rio Grande?

a. Meriwether Lewis and William Clark
b. Zebulon Pike
c. Henry Clay
d. Toussaint L'Overture

2. For what reason did the United States become involved in the War of 1812?

a. The United States wanted its independence from England.
b. United States citizens were determined to gain freedom of religion.
c. United States citizens wanted the British to cease interfering with their trading laws.
d. Americans wanted the British to cease colonizing the United States of America.

71

3. What was a major result of the Industrial Revolution?

    a. A decrease in large-scale manufacturing

    b. The development of the factory system

    c. The growth of rural areas

    d. The increase in imported commodities, rather than American-produced materials

4. The Civil Rights Act of 1866 granted the right of citizenship to all people of the United States EXCEPT...

    a. African Americans.

    b. European Americans.

    c. Asian Americans.

    d. Native Americans.

5. Which of the following was NOT a reason President Andrew Johnson was impeached in 1867?

    a. He insisted that the new state governments in the South ratify the 13th Amendment abolishing slavery.

    b. He gave ex-Confederate military officers and large plantation owners official government pardons.

    c. He vetoed the bill for the Civil Rights Act.

    d. He allowed ex-Confederates to serve as military commanders in the South.

6. Which of the following is NOT a reason the South seceded from the Union in 1861?

    a. The election of Abraham Lincoln

    b. The Southern States believed their state rights were being violated.

    c. Slaves started an Underground Railroad.

    d. The South did not like the North infringing on southern trade.

7. Which of the following states did NOT secede from the United States at the start of the Civil War?

    a. South Carolina

    b. Maryland

    c. North Carolina

    d. Virginia

8. During the Reconstruction after the Civil War, the Southerners had animosity toward the "carpetbaggers" because they...

    a. Traveled from the North to take advantage of financial opportunities in the devastated South.

    b. Convinced the newly-freed slaves to run for political office.

    c. Took advantage of newly-impoverished plantation owners to gain land and political power.

    d. All of the above

9. Which of the following battles was fought during the Civil War?

    a. Battle of Bunker Hill

    b. Battle of Yorktown

    c. Battle of the Bulge

    d. Battle of Antietam

10. Which of the following groups of American citizens gained suffrage first?

a. Women
b. Native Americans
c. African-American men
d. African-American women

11. Who among the following was NOT a President of the United States?

a. Benjamin Franklin
b. Benjamin Harrison
c. Rutherford B. Hayes
d. Chester A. Arthur

Economics

1. Under which of the following economic models does the United States of America operate?

a. Socialist system
b. Barter system
c. Capitalist system
d. Communist system

2. Water, time, and raw materials are all examples of what?

a. Products
b. Liquid assets
c. Common goods
d. Commodities

3. A fall in the value of a currency coupled with an overall increase in prices is also called a(n)...

a. Economic crisis.
b. Inflation.
c. Stock market collapse.
d. Recession.

4. The dollar value of all goods and services a country produces in a year is measured in which of the following terms?

a. Quality of life
b. A country's natural resources
c. Gross domestic product
d. Profit

5. If a product were highly desired, the concept of supply and demand would dictate that prices would...

a. Rise.
b. Remain stagnant.
c. Fluctuate inconsistently.
d. None of the above

73

6. The federal government providing purchasing incentives for electric car buyers is an example of what?

    a. Subsidy
    b. Mandate
    c. Stipulation
    d. Change in demand

7. What is an interest rate?

    a. The level of consumer appeal an organization has at a given moment
    b. A factor that motivates and influences the behavior of an individual
    c. The value of a good or service
    d. A percentage paid for the ability to borrow money over a specified amount of time

8. Companies can protect ideas and products from competitors by using which of the following?

    a. Reservation
    b. Copyright
    c. Entrepreneurship
    d. Quota

9. The activity of buying and selling is known as what?

    a. Commerce
    b. Business
    c. Shopping
    d. Collateral

Vocabulary

Have you ever stopped to think about just how important words are? Virtually every interaction you'll ever have with other human beings will involve words, either written or spoken. Whether you're at home or at school, on the playground or visiting a sick relative at the hospital, you'll use words to communicate your thoughts to others, and they'll do the same.

The bigger your vocabulary, the better your communication skills will be. Knowing the meanings of lots of words allows you to be more precise, be more descriptive, and write and speak better in many different ways. You'll also be able to understand others better, which will enable you to connect with them on a deeper level. Building your vocabulary is a life-long process, because you will never stop having the opportunity to learn new words. The following exercise will help you improve your vocabulary.

For each sentence, choose the answer that is the closest in meaning to the word in italics.

1. Geri's dad works as a *chauffeur*.

- a. Head cook at a restaurant
- b. limousine driver
- c. college professor
- d. massage therapist

2. The differences between the two are *trivial*.

- a. not important
- b. extremely important
- c. confusing
- d. hard to explain

3. The *monologue* was the best part of the play.

- a. scenery
- b. musical score
- c. long speech
- d. medieval costume

4. That stuff is really *toxic*.

- a. expensive
- b. fast acting
- c. poisonous
- d. effective

5. They will probably *confiscate* his passport.

- a. stamp
- b. reissue
- c. ignore
- d. take away

6. Mrs. Jones is a very *fastidious* client.

- a. hard to please
- b. friendly
- c. talkative
- d. easily satisfied

7. It was a very *lavish* party.

   a. boring
   b. crowded
   c. expensive
   d. lasting a long time

8. My dad *conceived* the original plans.

   a. copied
   b. lost
   c. improved
   d. came up with

9. I found him to be quite *amiable*.

   a. friendly
   b. forgetful
   c. rude
   d. angry

10. In her later years, she became a *recluse*.

   a. a person who reads a lot
   b. a famous person
   c. a person who moves from place to place
   d. a person who prefers to be alone

11. Are those birds *migratory*?

   a. subsisting on dead animals
   b. moving to a new place when the season changes
   c. lacking the ability to fly
   d. making their home near bodies of water

12. There are several *barriers* between here and there.

   a. tall, round containers
   b. rest areas
   c. signposts giving directions
   d. things that makes something difficult

13. Our high school football team has a *surfeit* of talent.

   a. just the right amount
   b. a huge amount
   c. not quite enough
   d. far too little

14. Their business practices are *predatory*.

   a. highly skilled
   b. harmful to others
   c. ineffective
   d. well known

15. That was a *raucous* gathering last night.

   a. very enjoyable
   b. very long
   c. very loud
   d. very crowded

16. Bobby's shirt and pants are *saturated*.

   a. fashionable
   b. mismatched
   c. out of date
   d. completely wet

17. Her behavior at the party was *contemptible*.

   a. unworthy of respect
   b. strange or odd
   c. highly admirable
   d. hilarious

18. We were very impressed with your *maneuver*.

   a. educational background
   b. skillful movement
   c. short speech
   d. complete redesign

19. His actions resulted in *turmoil*.

   a. a decisive victory
   b. a bad infection
   c. a staggering loss
   d. a great disturbance

20. That fabric is very *durable*.

   a. strong
   b. soft
   c. fragile
   d. pretty

21. The prosecution's evidence was *irrefutable*.

   a. extremely confusing
   b. poorly organized
   c. impossible to disprove
   d. not very convincing

22. When it comes to work, Tom moves at a *glacial* pace.

   a. average
   b. extremely fast
   c. uneven
   d. extremely slow

23. Sharice will be in charge of designing the *interior* of the piece.

    a. top
    b. bottom
    c. inside
    d. outside

24. The late king's nephew *usurped* the throne from his son.

    a. seized unlawfully
    b. bought the rights to
    c. inherited
    d. defended

25. Mrs. Barnes has an *unorthodox* approach to teaching.

    a. unusual
    b. uninteresting
    c. unacceptable
    d. undeveloped

26. Sometimes my uncle acts like a *barbarian*.

    a. a person studying to become a barber
    b. a person who drinks a lot of alcohol
    c. someone whose behavior is uncivilized
    d. a person who reads a lot

27. In the parade, the VFW's float will *precede* the high school's float.

    a. go at the same time
    b. go before
    c. go after
    d. be more popular than

28. The riddle was *insoluble*.

    a. easy to solve
    b. hilarious
    c. impossible to solve
    d. written in invisible ink

29. There was a click, and suddenly his voice was *audible*.

    a. able to be heard
    b. unable to be heard
    c. high-pitched
    d. low-pitched

30. The author is attempting to *obscure* the truth.

    a. announce
    b. hide
    c. make fun of
    d. discover

31. The seating arrangement was *haphazard*.

- a. rectangular
- b. round
- c. forming a perfect square
- d. disorganized

32. Can anyone explain how the *discrepancy* came about?

- a. argument between two people
- b. two things that should match up but don't
- c. a physical fight between two people
- d. something that's extremely embarrassing

33. His *exuberance* is understandable.

- a. energetic enthusiasm
- b. unwillingness to do something
- c. eagerness to make friends
- d. extreme hunger

34. Her *melancholy* seems to come and go.

- a. upset stomach
- b. unexplained sadness
- c. ability to get along with others
- d. restlessness

35. You'll need to *adapt* the recipe.

- a. print
- b. discard
- c. adjust
- d. create

36. My little brother is so *obnoxious*!

- a. cute
- b. smart for his age
- c. growing fast
- d. annoying

37. My slippers getting chewed by the puppy was *inevitable*.

- a. very sad
- b. unforgivable
- c. outrageous
- d. unavoidable

38. The old lady looked very *serene* in her bed.

- a. calm
- b. wrinkled
- c. upset
- d. near death

39. The weatherman *revised* his forecast.

    a. announced
    b. changed
    c. wrote down
    d. planned

40. I found the service at that hotel to be *inferior*.

    a. high in quality
    b. low in quality
    c. average in quality
    d. very fast

41. The interviewer was not impressed with Matt's *attire*.

    a. attitude
    b. conversation
    c. clothing
    d. hairstyle

Spelling

Being good at spelling goes hand in hand with being successful in school, and, when you're older, it will be important for success in a career. In today's world of texting and instant messaging, it's easy to get the impression that good spelling skills no longer matter much at all. That impression is false, though. Good spelling skills will always be important, and anyone who isn't a good speller will have to overcome more hurdles to be successful than other people. Like it or not, you will be judged your whole life by your spelling skills. The good news is that spelling is an area in which it's actually quite easy to get better with just a little practice. This section will help you improve your spelling skills.

Spelling Exercise

Each question contains four words for you to consider. If one of them is misspelled, circle it. If they are all spelled correctly, circle NO MISTAKES.

1.	visible	collision	ballut	chauffeur	NO MISTAKES
2.	overwelming	endure	arrival	democracy	NO MISTAKES
3.	evident	accumpany	banana	cleanse	NO MISTAKES
4.	rubbish	broccoli	vaxination	seize	NO MISTAKES
5.	grieve	shepard	exception	gazelle	NO MISTAKES
6.	version	inane	technician	suvenere	NO MISTAKES
7.	moralle	obesity	throughout	acquittal	NO MISTAKES
8.	amfibian	turmoil	galaxy	merely	NO MISTAKES
9.	celebrate	scolar	recognition	nuisance	NO MISTAKES
10.	innocent	mortgage	newmonia	medicine	NO MISTAKES
11.	brochure	reprimand	urgent	rithum	NO MISTAKES
12.	fatigue	peediatrician	oasis	authority	NO MISTAKES
13.	monitter	operator	abandon	participate	NO MISTAKES
14.	respectively	psychiatrist	irate	confiskate	NO MISTAKES
15.	abbreviate	knitted	imobilize	comparison	NO MISTAKES
16.	hospitable	unison	emphasis	solutary	NO MISTAKES
17.	merchendice	sanitary	leisurely	strengthen	NO MISTAKES
18.	anachronism	regurjitate	grueling	abrupt	NO MISTAKES
19.	analysis	usurp	endulge	wholly	NO MISTAKES
20.	indeuce	category	repugnant	inaugural	NO MISTAKES
21.	gaseous	civilization	laborious	exude	NO MISTAKES
22.	fastidious	dalinquent	accumulate	protocol	NO MISTAKES
23.	rapport	obscure	eminent	counterfit	NO MISTAKES
24.	jeopardize	inscription	clientell	siege	NO MISTAKES
25.	reputable	pleeted	raspberry	catastrophe	NO MISTAKES
26.	embaras	luxurious	zoology	mimic	NO MISTAKES
27.	decafinated	procedure	alumni	perjury	NO MISTAKES
28.	simultaneous	concentrate	cullprit	flexible	NO MISTAKES
29.	ocasional	bacterial	distinguished	rigid	NO MISTAKES
30.	committed	lopsided	serennity	jewelry	NO MISTAKES
31.	disability	forfeit	strenuous	labaratory	NO MISTAKES
32.	knowledgeable	generous	adhere	ajerned	NO MISTAKES
33.	publicity	duplicate	recuring	ransack	NO MISTAKES
34.	kerosene	flamboyant	boyant	unique	NO MISTAKES

Capitalization

Capital letters are very important in written English. They can be used to show respect to people, to identify certain things, and to show that a new sentence has begun. Some words, such as *February* or *Jupiter*, need to be capitalized every time you use them. Other words, like *judge* or *doctor*, are only capitalized in certain situations. For this reason, there are rules to help you remember which words need capitalization. Capitalization can be confusing, so a good rule of thumb is that words are capitalized if they refer to unique persons, places or things (nouns), if they start a sentence, or if they are part of a person's or thing's title.

Some quick capitalization rules – all these should be capitalized:

- The first word of every sentence
- The first word of a quote
- Names of persons, months, days, holidays, countries, states, and cities
- Initials used in names and well-known organizations
- The word "I"
- Titles of books, songs, or people

This exercise will help you improve your capitalization skills. For each numbered item, read each sentence, and then decide if all of them are capitalized correctly, or if one is capitalized incorrectly. If one of the sentences is capitalized incorrectly, select the letter of the sentence which contains the mistake. If all of them are capitalized correctly, choose NO MISTAKES. Sentences may contain words that aren't capitalized that should be, words that are capitalized that shouldn't be, or both.

1.
   a. My mom and dad are both six feet tall.
   b. We went shopping for clothes at the Mall.
   c. Tomorrow is Groundhog Day.
   d. NO MISTAKES

2.
   a. I know all the words to the star-spangled banner.
   b. My sister sang a solo in church yesterday.
   c. We attend St. Mark's Episcopal Church, which is downtown.
   d. NO MISTAKES

3.
   a. Did Charlie Chaplin ever win an Academy Award?
   b. My ancestors came to America on the Mayflower.
   c. Francis Scott Key wrote the lyrics to the National Anthem.
   d. NO MISTAKES

4.
   a. My cousin will start his Military Career at fort Leonard Wood.
   b. When I was younger, I loved going to Chuck E. Cheese for pizza.
   c. London is the biggest city in England.
   d. NO MISTAKES

5.

   a. I think he's got a good shot at being named rookie of the year.
   b. That pitcher is doing quite well for a rookie.
   c. I always root for the National League in the All-Star Game.
   d. NO MISTAKES

6.

   a. My Fair Lady is a very funny play.
   b. He had memorized the Multiplication Table by age 4.
   c. I think Tom Hanks is the Best Actor in the history of Hollywood.
   d. NO MISTAKES

7.

   a. This summer, we're going to Montreal, Canada to visit my sister.
   b. Last summer was the hottest one on record, according to the National Weather Service.
   c. Our family goes to six flags over Texas every summer.
   d. NO MISTAKES

8.

   a. There are 66 books in the bible.
   b. There are thousands of books in a small library.
   c. The New York Public Library contains millions of books.
   d. NO MISTAKES

9.

   a. The Battle of Little Bighorn is also known as Custer's Last Stand.
   b. General Eisenhower led the American forces in World War II.
   c. Man, it sounds like there's a War going on in the gym!
   d. NO MISTAKES

10.

   a. My neighbor speaks French fluently.
   b. My dad teaches Spanish Language and Literature 101 at the college.
   c. The Russian Language is one of the most difficult to learn.
   d. NO MISTAKES

11.

   a. We found the missing puppy at the corner of Maple Avenue and Oak Street.
   b. We called the number on the flyer on the Bulletin Board at Kroger.
   c. The Jones family tried to give us a reward, but we refused to take it.
   d. NO MISTAKES

12.

   a. Many people think Television was invented in 1947, but that is incorrect.
   b. A lot of Mom's favorite TV shows are on the Food Network.
   c. In 2008, the History Channel changed its name to History.
   d. NO MISTAKES

13.

    a. February 14th is Valentine's Day.

    b. Christmas falls on December 25th.

    c. My Birthday is July 17th.

    d. NO MISTAKES

14.

    a. Fred and Barney are the names of my cats.

    b. I named them after the flintstones characters.

    c. It was a popular animated show on television in the 1960's.

    d. NO MISTAKES

15.

    a. The official deadline is 11:59 PM Central Standard Time.

    b. What time is the meeting next Tuesday?

    c. We need to leave no later than Noon.

    d. NO MISTAKES

16.

    a. We watched the game between the Detroit Lions and the Chicago Bears.

    b. Last year I went and saw the Indianapolis Colts play the Jacksonville Jaguars.

    c. At the zoo I saw Lions, Bears, and Jaguars.

    d. NO MISTAKES

17.

    a. Officers with the Hulbert Municipal Police Department made the arrest last night.

    b. Sheriff Johnson assisted the police department in locating the suspect.

    c. Robert Johnson has been the sheriff for over 25 years now.

    d. NO MISTAKES

18.

    a. The First Amendment protects our right to engage in free speech.

    b. This is the first amendment the city council has made to the zoning law in over 20 years.

    c. Class, how many amendments to the Constitution are there?

    d. NO MISTAKES

19.

    a. There are three breeds of Ducks at the park: Muscovy, Ancona, and Pekin.

    b. We love watching the ducks when we go to Mt. Hope Park.

    c. The ducks at the park are very friendly and unafraid of humans.

    d. NO MISTAKES

20.

    a. We went to the Museum of Modern Art when we visited New York City.

    b. I didn't care for most of the Art Pieces on display in that museum.

    c. I prefer traditional art, such as the works of Van Gogh or Rembrandt.

    d. NO MISTAKES

21.

   a. It's traditional to sing Auld Lang Syne on New Year's Eve.

   b. Have you made any resolutions for the coming New Year?

   c. Happy New Year!

   d. NO MISTAKES

22.

   a. My mom is a republican, but my dad is a democrat.

   b. My dad is Lutheran, but my mom is Baptist.

   c. My mom is from Ohio, but my dad's a Hoosier.

   d. NO MISTAKES

23.

   a. Officer Menendez has been recognized for bravery three times.

   b. If you see something suspicious, call the Police at once.

   c. My uncle was named Officer of the Year by the Huntsville Police Department.

   d. NO MISTAKES

24.

   a. Doesn't everybody love pumpkin pie?

   b. In my opinion, Everybody Loves Raymond was the best show ever.

   c. I hope my pumpkin pie takes 1st Prize at this year's Pumpkin Festival.

   d. NO MISTAKES

25.

   a. The letters in YMCA stand for Young Men's Christian Association.

   b. I like reading everything I can find about the nba or the nfl.

   c. Many people in China follow Confucianism.

   d. NO MISTAKES

26.

   a. Dr. Seuss wasn't a real Doctor.

   b. Doctor Jones will see you now, Mr. Williams.

   c. Ph.D stands for Doctor of Philosophy.

   d. NO MISTAKES

27.

   a. Henry, have you seen my copy of Time magazine?

   b. It's high time Congress passed the spending bill.

   c. Professor, do you think we'll ever be able to go backward in Time?

   d. NO MISTAKES

Punctuation

Correct punctuation is a critical part of written communications. Imagine trying to read a book with no periods. It would be unpleasant, to say the least. For example, periods tell us when we've come to the end of a complete thought, so we mentally take a very brief pause before moving on to the next thought. This is very important for helping us understand and retain what we've read. The same principle holds true for all punctuation. Every comma, colon, semicolon, dash, question mark, etc., makes it easier to read and comprehend the text. By the same token, missing or incorrect punctuation can confuse the reader.

The text in each question may contain a punctuation error. If there is an error, select the answer choice which contains the error. If there is no error, select NO MISTAKES.

1.

    a.   It's very late; we'd better call it a night.
    b.   Mom and Dad are tired (we're heading home).
    c.   Since it's clear our team is going to lose, we're leaving early to beat the traffic.
    d.   NO MISTAKES

2.

    a.   Well, that's easy for you to say.
    b.   All's well, that ends well.
    c.   Well done, sir.
    d.   NO MISTAKES

3.

    a.   This is the funniest book I've ever read.
    b.   That's strange; it was here a minute ago.
    c.   Zach and Sally you will be lab partners.
    d.   NO MISTAKES

4.

    a.   Dad said – to ask you to make a grocery list.
    b.   That's right – today is Mom's birthday!
    c.   He said – and I quote – "Don't worry about it."
    d.   NO MISTAKES

5.

    a.   For whom, does the bell toll?
    b.   What are you referring to, Jackie?
    c.   If you want, we can ride our bikes down to the creek.
    d.   NO MISTAKES

6.

    a.   I have never missed a day of school (except snow days).
    b.   She won the 1st place trophy in her age group (14 and under) at last year's fair.
    c.   Mrs. Garcia said there will be a test (on Friday).
    d.   NO MISTAKES

7.

    a. Who said, "All's fair in love and war", Heather?
    b. "These are the times that try men's souls" is a famous quote.
    c. My kitten is "six months old" today.
    d. NO MISTAKES

8.

    a. These are the team captains: Jake, Shelley, Frannie, and Tom.
    b. These are the team captains; Jake, Shelley, Frannie, and Tom.
    c. The team captains are Jake, Shelley, Frannie, and Tom.
    d. NO MISTAKES

9.

    a. The blacksmith's anvil is often used as a metaphor.
    b. The Smith's oldest son just graduated from law school.
    c. The law school's website says it's one of the top schools in the nation.
    d. NO MISTAKES

10.

    a. The class motto is "Striving for Excellence".
    b. And then the umpire said, "One more outburst and I'll eject you."
    c. "To be, or not to be," Shakespeare said, "that is the question."
    d. NO MISTAKES

11.

    a. Mary, I'd like a word with you after class.
    b. The teacher asked Mary, who had been interrupting, to stay after class.
    c. The teacher, asked Mary who had been interrupting, to stay after class.
    d. NO MISTAKES

12.

    a. If you're going to do something why not do it right the first time?
    b. It's just a hop, skip, and a jump from here.
    c. Let's start over.
    d. NO MISTAKES

13.

    a. My neighbor is a truck driver who's on the road a lot so I rarely see him.
    b. My neighbor is a truck driver so he's gone a lot.
    c. My neighbor is on the road a lot because he's a truck driver.
    d. NO MISTAKES

14.

    a. "Have it your way," sighed the waiter, exasperated.
    b. Suddenly he asked, "What time is it?"
    c. "Congratulations, class! Everyone passed!" proclaimed Mr. Henderson.
    d. NO MISTAKES

15.

    a. The clown smiled waved and took a deep bow.
    b. I enjoy going to the circus; it's very entertaining.
    c. Although I enjoy the circus, I have no desire to become a clown.
    d. NO MISTAKES

16.

    a. You should teach your dog some fun tricks.
    b. I'm teaching my dog Buddy how to sit up and beg.
    c. Last week I taught him to "speak."
    d. NO MISTAKES

17.

    a. Unfortunately for our team, the other team scored six runs in the ninth inning.
    b. The other team scored; six runs in the ninth inning.
    c. That's the sixth run they've scored this inning!
    d. NO MISTAKES

18.

    a. Don't worry about it; it's really not that important.
    b. Kids, study hard in school, because the future will be here, before you know it.
    c. You'll turn into a middle-aged adult so fast it will make your head spin.
    d. NO MISTAKES

19.

    a. Be that as it may we should delay the vote until all members are present.
    b. Nothing doing, pal!
    c. Who do you think will win the championship, Bobby?
    d. NO MISTAKES

20.

    a. Jack, having a previous engagement, declined our invitation.
    b. Did Jack really say "I can't make it tonight?"
    c. "I'm sorry, guys, but I can't make it tonight," were his exact words.
    d. NO MISTAKES

21.

    a. Wooden blocks can be both fun and educational for toddlers.
    b. Marie, aren't you a little old to be playing with wooden blocks?
    c. Actually I find playing with wooden blocks to be a great way of relaxing.
    d. NO MISTAKES

22.

    a. Too many people take the 'lesser of two evils' approach to voting.
    b. Millions of people don't bother voting at all.
    c. When you vote – and you should always vote – you play an important role in governing.
    d. NO MISTAKES

23.

    a. "Now is the time for all good men to come to the aid of their country."
    b. Am I dreaming or has school really been canceled due to snow?
    c. Fool me once, shame on you; fool me twice, shame on me.
    d. NO MISTAKES

24.

    a. The quick brown, fox jumps over the lazy dog.
    b. Facebook is one of the most popular websites in the entire world.
    c. The phrase "ETAOIN SHRDLU" is a meaningless phrase made from the twelve most used letters.
    d. NO MISTAKES

25.

    a. His mother said gently, "Henry, I'm afraid it's time for us to go home."
    b. "It's your move, sir," said my opponent.
    c. Mom said and this is an exact quote, "No way, Jose!"
    d. NO MISTAKES

26.

    a. Did you ever, see such a thing?
    b. Have you ever heard of such a thing?
    c. Doesn't that just beat all, Grandpa?
    d. NO MISTAKES

27.

    a. On your mark, get set, go!
    b. Once bitten, twice shy.
    c. Easy come easy go.
    d. NO MISTAKES

Practice Test Answers and Explanations

Reading

1. C: In the first sentence in paragraph 2, it is stated that "Saturday was the day Adventure Land was opening." In paragraph 1, the narrator explains that she is excited and later states that Saturday is her friend's birthday, but the first reason given is that Adventure Land is opening.

2. D: The narrator provides many examples of her excitement throughout paragraph 3, such as that she could not sleep and was not listening to her mom because she was thinking about all of the fun things she was going to do.

3. A: The narrator begins the essay by stating that she was looking forward to Saturday, and the following paragraphs explain why. Although other elements are explained, the main focus is why Saturday is exciting.

4. B: Words like "vines" and "safari" bring about images that reflect the jungle. The narrator explained that the amusement park was decorated in the theme of the jungle and used these words to help create the image.

5. B: Paragraph 5 explains that Riley's mom wanted the children to stay with their buddies, and in paragraph 6, Riley's mom tells the children what to do if they get lost. If the children stayed with their buddy, there was less of a chance of someone getting lost.

6. D: In paragraph 12, the narrator states that since it was her friend's birthday, they were allowed to ride in the front seats.

7. A: The narrator mentions being lost several times throughout the essay, and the central conflict is when the children think someone is lost. The narrator explains that there are many people in the park to create an image that it would be easy to get lost, which would be bad.

8. C: Paragraphs 17-26 explain the conflict the children have when they think someone is lost. They become very worried and try to find George. The narrator mentions earlier that Riley's mother did not want anyone lost, and so the conflict is to find the lost friend.

9. B: Natalie was with George and the children assume that she was his buddy. In paragraph 6, Riley's mother states that if anyone gets lost, they should go to the food court. Since George is lost, the children assume he must have gone to the food court.

10. C: Bewildered means to become confused. Since the children were expecting George to be a person, they were confused to find a stuffed animal.

11. A: The conflict of the story is trying to find George, who is lost. The conflict is resolved when George is found.

12. D: The children were worried because they thought of one their friends was lost. They were surprised to discover that they had been searching for a stuffed animal and not a person.

13. C: The author assumes that audiences will hope the lovers can be saved. This is not a fact. Choices A, B, and D are all facts that are supported by information in the play.

90

14. D: Paragraph 5 states that the prologue is in the first moments of the play.

15. B: Paragraph 2 explains all of the information that is in the prologue, and the author says that the prologue provides the plot of the play. The conflict is also explained in discussing the feud between the families.

16. A: Feud means disagreement, argument, or fight.

17. B: Paragraphs 6 and 7 explain that the author believes that even though they watch a play with the understanding that it will be tragic, they continue to watch it because they hope it will end happily.

18. C: Evidence means providing help to reveal truth or proof. The prologue provides evidence that the play will not end happily.

19. A: In paragraph 3, the author states that most people expect and enjoy a happy ending as they have grown up with stories that end happily with the phrase, "And they lived happily ever after."

20. D: In paragraph 4, the author explains that Juliet faked her death and that Romeo does not receive the message.

21. B: In paragraph 5, the author explains that it is interesting to explain at the beginning of the play that Romeo and Juliet die and that their deaths end their parents' feud.

22. C: In paragraph 2, the narrator explains that the prologue states that Romeo and Juliet take their lives and in doing so, end their parents' feud.

23. C: Personification is giving human traits to non-human objects. Wind, an object and not a person, cannot whisper.

24. D: A simile compares two things by using the words "like" or "as". The author compares the rain to rivers by using the word, "like".

25. B: "Mother" is a proper noun because it is referring to a unique name, rather than a common noun. "Mother" in the poem is used as a name, which is why it is capitalized.

26. A: Paragraph 1 discusses how Gibson was named and that he was born into music. Paragraph 2 discusses music within his parent's lives. Paragraph 3 discusses how he came to play instruments.

27. D: The story is third-person limited as it is not told in the first-person, by Gibson or any other character, and the narrator only knows the thoughts and feelings of one character, Gibson.

28. B: Paragraph 4 states that Gibson's family had just moved from Seattle, which explains that he is a new student in the school.

29. A: Paragraph 1 discusses music in Gibson's life and the fact that he was born into music through his family and even his name. He thinks that it was the music that chose him, and because of this, he "never really had a chance" to not have music be very involved in his life.

30. C: In paragraph 3, it is stated that Gibson's favorite instrument was also the one he had been playing the longest, his father's Gibson Les Paul guitar.

31. B: The narrator explains that Gibson wanted to stay in his seat and have no one look at him. He did not want the attention of the other children.

91

32. D: From the beginning of the essay, the narrator states that music was always a part of Gibson's life and helped shaped his interests. The essay moves into discussing Gibson at a new school, and eventually how his love of music helps him to be himself at school.

33. A: The conflict in the story is that as a new student, Gibson is teased by his fellow classmates. By showing his love of music as well as his talent, Gibson is himself and is liked by his classmates.

34. D: The main argument is stated in paragraph 4: "With the progression and extreme convenience of technology, printed books are going to soon become a thing of the past."

35. C: Paragraph 1 explains how stories have progressed, beginning with oral tradition and past the invention of the printing press. In context with the rest of the essay, this paragraph is important in explaining how stories progress and are provided within society.

36. B: Enduring means to put up with something unpleasant. Within the sentence, the phrase, "enduring a several hour flight," the word enduring, means to undergo.

37. A: In paragraph 1, it is stated that oral tradition was the main medium for storytelling before the invention of the printing press.

38. C: In paragraph 2, it is stated that reliance on books for information was changed with the invention of the Internet.

39. B: It is not a fact that "sliding a finger across the screen or pressing a button to move onto the next page is just as satisfying to the reader." Satisfaction is not something universal that can be proven for every reader. This statement is an opinion.

40. A: The author makes the argument in paragraph 5 that devices such as the iPad and Kindle are "therefore better than books because they have multiple uses."

41. D: In the beginning of the essay, the author explains how stories were passed through oral tradition. This was changed by the printing press, which is becoming less important with technology and the invention of the Internet and devices such as the iPad and Kindle.

42. C: A categorical claim is an arguable understanding of facts, rather than an absolute fact. The statement regarding the qualities of the iPad and Kindle is the only statement that is a fact.

43. D: Paragraph 1 states that Aberystwyth is located on the West Coast of Wales.

44. C: The essay provides information on various aspects of the town of Aberystwyth, providing a portrait of the town as a whole.

45. A: Situated means to be placed in a certain location.

46. B: In an essay that is factual, proclaiming that the scenery is "gorgeous" or that a town is a "hidden luxury" is an opinion.

47. B: Paragraph 3 states that two main languages are traditionally spoken in Aberystwyth.

48. C: Paragraph 1 states, "A market town refers to European areas that have the right to have markets, which differentiates it from a city or village."

49. D: Paragraph 2 states, "Constitution Hill is a hill on the north end of Aberystwyth, which provides excellent views of Cardigan Bay and which is supported by the Aberystwyth Electric Cliff Railway."

50. A: Paragraph 1 explains that Aberystwyth is best known as an education center, and this is repeated in paragraph 3, which states that Aberystwyth is best known for its educational services.

Written Expression

1. D: This stanza talks about how the woman's beauty remains constant, despite differences in her appearance that are due to the light. Her beauty is present in all her physical aspects. The line that precedes the ones related to this question is: *Or softly lightens o'er her face;*. The semicolon at the end of this line tells the reader that the speaker's thought is not yet finished, and that what follows is directly related to what has just been mentioned: the woman's face.

2. A: Looking at the last words in each line of the first stanza reveals the following rhyme scheme: A (night) B (skies) A (bright) B (eyes) A (light) B (denies). This pattern is repeated in the other two stanzas.

3. C: The repetition of the "c" and "s" sounds in this line is an example of alliteration. Personification is the application of human characteristics to something that is not human. A rhyming couplet needs two lines, and a quatrain is a four-line stanza.

4. C: Images of dark and light can be found throughout the first two stanzas, and are always described as enhancing or complimenting beauty. It doesn't matter whether the woman is in darkness or light; she is beautiful.

5. A: This is the most likely choice, as the information provided gives more insight into what was going on in the author's mind. It would not likely cause the reader to form an opinion about the woman herself, nor does it give clues about the season during which the poem takes place or the identity of the author.

6. A: Lily's dislike of Rosedale is apparent in this passage. She is worried that he will tell others that she was exiting Selden's apartment building, and is concerned about what social consequences that might have for her: *Lily was sure that within twenty-four hours the story of her visiting her dressmaker at the Benedick would be in active circulation among Mr. Rosedale's acquaintances.*

7. B: All of the details that are given about people and events are presented from Lily's point of view. They are not objective, and reflect her reactions and opinions.

8. D: This detail comes from Lily's internal dialogue. The reader is privy to this since the story is told from her perspective. Everything is filtered through her perspective and knowledge. As a viewer of a film portrayal, this perspective is completely changed from that of a participant to that of an observer. The scene could plainly depict the details in answers A through C, but the detail in answer D is part of Lily's internal analysis, which would not be part of a film scene.

9. D: This part of the passage talks about how Jack Stepney keeps bringing Rosedale to fashionable places and events, and how he is snubbed for his actions. Rosedale is snubbed, too. Yet, he persists, saying "You'll see" to the naysayers. The answers that focus on Rosedale are incorrect, and there is no discussion of violence, as "sticking to one's guns" is used figuratively here.

10. C: The places where Rosedale's race is referenced and the line cited in this question allude to anti-Semitic attitudes toward the man.

11. B: Lincoln begins this speech by discussing the founding of our country and what the original purpose of the U.S. was. Then, he goes on to talk about how the U.S. is currently engaged in a war intended to fracture the nation, and he states that the battle being discussed was one large tragedy that came out of the war. Next, Lincoln says that his speech and even the memorial itself can't truly honor those who died, and that it's up to those who survived to continue the fight to ensure the nation does not break apart. Answer B best communicates this message.

12. C: The sentence in which this phrase is found is: *The world will little note, nor long remember, what we say here, but can never forget what they did here.* In this context, the phrase "the world will little note" means that no one outside of those in attendance or possibly those outside the country will pay attention to the speech or the ceremony. This eliminates all of the answer choices except C.

13. A: The ideals of the revolution are addressed in the first paragraph: Four score and seven years ago our fathers brought forth, upon this continent, a new nation, conceived in Liberty, and dedicated to the proposition that all men are created equal. This introduces the point that Lincoln is trying to make about the battle at hand and the war as a whole: the Civil War is threatening the ideas upon which the nation was created.

14. C: There is a comparison between the ideas of the Revolution and the Civil War in this speech. To facilitate understanding of this comparison, Lincoln has to set the stage by telling his audience about the past event he is referencing. This establishes the context of his message.

15. A: This line directly references the idea in the previous paragraph, which is that the U.S. is a nation that was created to ensure liberty and equality. This sentence talks about how the Civil War is testing whether or not a nation that was created to ensure liberty and equality can really survive.

16. A: Emerson writes that love "unites [man] to his race... and gives permanence to human society." None of the other sentiments are addressed in the first paragraph.

17. C: Emerson addresses age in the second paragraph and in this sentence: The natural association of the sentiment of love with the heyday of the blood seems to require that in order to portray it in vivid tints, which every youth and maid should confess to be true to their throbbing experience, one must not be too old. What he means is that the extreme passion of love is usually felt and pursued by the young.

18. B: In this sentence from the second paragraph, Emerson discusses how love is favored by the young, but is also a significant part of the lives of those who are no longer "young." This sentence in particular talks about how love begins as something small and personal, and grows until it is something large that unifies all people.

19. D: The text gives direct support and examples for this answer throughout the last seven sentences, starting with: *Everything is beautiful seen from the point of the intellect, or as truth. But all is sour, if seen as experience.*

20. D: This line from Allen's essay talks about love in relation to marriage, while the passage from Emerson's essay discusses the effects of love. None of the other answer choices fit.

21. A: This paragraph establishes that the U.S. Coast Guard is being discussed in an informational context. The other paragraphs provide supporting details.

22. D: Sentence 10 basically provides a laundry list of things that Coast Guard members do on a daily basis. The only answer choice that introduces this effectively is D.

23. A: Paragraph 3 gives information about what the Coast Guard does in an average day, but there is no indication as to where this very specific information comes from. Adding a line saying that the information came from the official Coast Guard Web site would add credibility.

24. C: This answer choice best sums up the information in this essay, and rounds out the writer's discussion about the organization as a whole. Answers A and B talk about the Coast Guard as a career, which isn't a theme in this essay. Answer D contradicts the information and ideas in the essay.

25. D: Publishing text through a blog is instantaneous and completely under the control of the author. The first two answer choices involve approaching other people and/or organizations to get them to publish the essay before the other steps are carried out. Answer C is probably the most complicated, since audio recording is involved. Answer D is the most efficient way to accomplish this task.

26. B: This source is the most reliable, and will provide the most relevant information. The other sources are either too broad or unrelated to the assigned topic.

27. A: The paragraph clearly shows the negative emotions that Brett was feeling during his mother's pregnancy. He wasn't indifferent about the situation, and he was not experiencing positive feelings about the pregnancy at this point. Answer A is the best choice.

28. B: Everything in this essay is filtered through Brett's perspective, even the dialogue he presents. The dialogue is used as an enhancement to Brett's thoughts, providing more of a humanizing touch to this memory. The other answer choices don't make sense.

29. D: The endearment helps soothe Brett's insecurities about a new baby being welcomed into the family.

30. C: Sentence 20 says: *I was scared, though.* In the context of this paragraph, this statement doesn't need to be made; it is implied. However, to understand the rest of what is being said, all of the other sentences are necessary.

31. D: The essay simply states that the birth of his sister was Brett's most memorable experience. It doesn't state why he feels this way.

32. A: Answer A connects back to the opening sentence in the essay and touches on the main theme of love, making it an appropriate way to conclude this writer's thoughts. The other answer choices don't really make sense in the context of what is being discussed in the final paragraph, or they do not convey the overall message of the essay.

33. D: This is the only fact. All of the other answer choices are opinions.

34. A: A history textbook would provide a more inclusive description of what was going on at the time of this speech, as well as specific details about the attack on Pearl Harbor.

35. C: Roosevelt makes a strong case for the declaration of war. He draws upon facts, and develops his argument in such a way that it communicates urgency without being irrational. Solid evidence and reasoning support his claim.

36. A: The gravestones in the background, the memorial plaque listing names under the words "attack on" in the foreground, the sad boy, and the American flags make answer A the most likely choice. The boy is not standing in front of a grave. There is no indication that there is any happiness associated with this event. But, there are enough clues in the picture to infer what is going on in the scene.

37. B: There is little about this scene that is happy or joyful, which makes answers A and C inappropriate. Though there is a seriousness to the scene, there is no indication that anyone is being reprimanded, or that there is any kind of extreme negative emotion here. The overall mood of this scene is reserved and respectful, which makes B the best choice.

38. D: Knowing that the boy has been personally affected by whatever events warranted this memorial shouldn't elicit negative emotions, but should provide a greater understanding of the boy's reaction. The new knowledge gives more information about him, and allows the viewer to better interpret the image based on that information.

39. A: Of the choices given, answer A is the only one that could spark a conversation that relies on a critical study of the image itself. Students would have to look at clues within the picture to determine what this memorial is all about, and would need to come up with reasons to back up their position.

40. C: There isn't really any indication that any sort of statement is being made with this picture. It is also not presenting information, as much of what is in the photo needs to be interpreted. Answer C is the best choice.

41. C: The subject of the sentence should be "Ben," but the noun that follows the comma at the end of the opening phrase names the subject as "the college Ben chose." This doesn't make sense, and is an example of a misplaced or dangling modifier. The subject, "the college Ben chose," agrees with the verb "was." "Harvard" is a noun, not a preposition.

42. C: An adverb is a word that modifies or describes a verb, an adjective, or another adverb. "Present" is a noun. "Wrapped" is a verb. "Professional" is a noun. "Expertly" is an adverb, and it modifies the verb "wrapped."

43. B: "Pervade" means to spread throughout or to be found throughout something. The sentence tells the reader that the excitement did something in the classroom. Answer B is the only one that makes sense.

44. A: "Fold" can be used to refer to a group, specifically a group of sheep, but also a group in general. When someone "enters the fold," they are literally or figuratively going along with a group.

45. C: Hyperventilation describes an excess of air. Hyperthermia describes an excess of heat.

46. D: The speaker's feelings are not clearly expressed in the first three answer choices. "Appreciated" and "issue" are abstract words, and saying that "Artie yelled" doesn't reveal how the speaker reacted. The reaction was probably negative, but we don't know that for sure. Answer D is the most descriptive. "Warm my heart" tells us that the gift meant something to the speaker, who is now feeling happy, loved, and affectionate.

47. B: The colon in this sentence correctly introduces a list of items. In answer A, the semicolon should be a comma. In answer C, there should be a question mark instead of a period. In answer D, the comma should be a semicolon.

48. A: Answer B should be "acclimate." Answer C should be "wizen." Answer D should be "allude."

49. C: A compound sentence contains two independent clauses joined with a coordinating conjunction. Answer A is a simple sentence. Answer B is a compound/complex sentence. Answer D is a complex sentence.

50. B: Dictionaries and glossaries provide definitions of words. Indexes tell you the page of a book or other work on which a topic is mentioned. A thesaurus is a reference for synonyms and antonyms.

Mathematics

1. B: The rational numbers for Choice B can be compared by either converting all of them to decimals or finding common denominators and comparing the newly written fractions. Using the first approach, the rational numbers shown for Choice B in order from left to right can be written as 6.4, 2.25, and 0.80. These numbers are indeed written in order from greatest to least. Also, the integer -2 is greater than -5. Thus, the numbers, $\frac{32}{5}, 2\frac{1}{4}, \frac{4}{5}, -2, -5$, are listed in order from greatest to least.

2. D: In order to convert the given fraction to a percentage, divide 2 by 7. Doing so gives a decimal of approximately 0.29. The decimal can be converted to a percentage by multiplying by 100, which moves the decimal point two places to the right and gives 29%.

3. C: The square has an area of 16 square units, with 4 units comprising the length of each side. Therefore, the square root of the area is 4.

4. B: The proportion can be written as $\frac{4}{2} = \frac{x}{18}$. Solving for x gives $x = 36$. Thus, there are 36 data analysis problems on the test.

5. D: In order to determine the amount available to each guest, the total amount of prepared lemonade should be divided by 25 guests. Thus, the expression $2\frac{1}{2} \div 25$ represents the amount that each guest has available for consumption. The mixed fraction can be rewritten as $\frac{5}{2}$. The expression can be simplified by writing $\frac{5}{2} \div 25 = \frac{5}{2} \times \frac{1}{25}$, which equals $\frac{5}{50}$, or $\frac{1}{10}$.

6. A: The number of one-fourths contained in $8\frac{1}{2}$ can be determined by dividing $8\frac{1}{2}$ by $\frac{1}{4}$. In order to find the quotient, $8\frac{1}{2}$ can be multiplied by the reciprocal of $\frac{1}{4}$, or 4. Thus, the quotient can be found by writing $\frac{17}{2} \times 4$, which equals 34.

7. A: The model shows that 4 is divided by sections equal to $\frac{3}{4}$ in length: $4 \div \frac{3}{4} = 5\frac{1}{3}$. The remaining piece that fits between $3\frac{3}{4}$ and 4 represents one-third of the length of each section. Thus, the quotient is $5\frac{1}{3}$.

8. D: The number line shows that 24 divided into 3 sections equals 8.

9. A: The number of hours traveled is equal to the ratio of the distance to the speed. Thus, the number of hours is equal to $\frac{840}{60}$, or 14.

Mømetrix

10. D: The cost per ounce can be calculated by dividing the cost of the bag by the number of ounces the bag contains. Thus, the cost per ounce can be calculated by writing $9.85 ÷ 16, which equals approximately $0.62 per ounce.

11. D: The order of operations states that numbers with exponents must be evaluated first. Thus, the expression can be rewritten as $64 + 12 ÷ 4 + 64 × 3$. Next, multiplication and division must be computed as they appear from left to right in the expression. Thus, the expression can be further simplified as $64 + 3 + 192$, which equals 259.

12. C: A table of values can be created to compare the amounts deposited each month by Amy and Douglas. During Month 7, Douglas deposits $64, while Amy only deposits $49. During the previous month (Month 6), Amy deposited $36, while Douglas deposited $32.

13. B: A donation of $110 per charity equals $1,430, which is more than Hannah plans to donate; thus, Choices A, C, and D are eliminated. A donation of $105 per charity equals $1,365 donated. A donation of $110 per charity equals $1,430. $1,400 is between $1,365 and $1,430; thus, she donated more than $105 but less than $110 to each charity.

14. B: The discounted price is 25% less than the original price. Therefore, the discounted price can be written as $36.95 − ((0.25)(36.95))$, which equals approximately 27.71. Thus, the discounted price of the jacket is $27.71.

15. B: In order to find the percentage discount, the following equation can be written: $36,549.15 = 42,999 − 42,999x$. The equation can be solved by writing: $36,549.15 − 42,999 = −42,999x$, which simplifies to $−6,449.85 = −42,999x$, with $x = 0.15$; therefore, the percent discount is 15%.

16. B: In order to find the unit rate, the cost of the bottle should be divided by the number of fluid ounces contained in the bottle: $\frac{\$3.96}{20} \approx 0.20$. Thus, the cost per fluid ounce is approximately $0.20.

17. B: The common difference, or slope, is −7. The value of the 18th term can be determined by finding the product of −7 and 18, which is −126. The equation $y = −7x$ can be used to find the value of any term in the sequence, where x represents the position number of the term.

18. C: Since the lengths of Triangle B are related to the lengths of Triangle A by a scale factor of $\frac{1}{4}$, each side length of Triangle A should be multiplied by the factor $\frac{1}{4}$: $12 × \frac{1}{4} = 3$; $8 × \frac{1}{4} = 2$; $16 × \frac{1}{4} = 4$. The side lengths of Triangle B measure 3 cm, 2 cm, and 4 cm, respectively.

19. B: One decimeter equals 10 centimeters, so The proportion can be written as: $\frac{1}{0.1} = \frac{x}{2.5}$. Solving for x gives $x = 25$. Thus, 2.5 decimeters is equal to 25 centimeters.

20. D: Based on the information given in the problem, for a sphere with a radius of 2 inches, the following equation can be written: $33.49 = 8\pi x$, where x represents the unknown ratio. Solving for x gives $x = \frac{4}{3}$. The ratio for a sphere with a radius of 4 inches can be determined using the equation $267.95 = 64\pi x$. Again, the ratio equals $\frac{4}{3}$. A check of each of the spheres shows the ratio to be $\frac{4}{3}$.

21. A: The graph shown for Choice A is the line $y = \frac{1}{3}x$, where both measurable quantities x and y are greater than or equal to zero Since 1 foot is one-third of a yard, this equation is representative of the relationship between number of feet and number of yards.

98

Copyright © Mometrix Media. You have been licensed one copy of this document for personal use only. Any other reproduction or redistribution is strictly prohibited. All rights reserved.
This content is provided for test preparation purposes only and does not imply an endorsement by Mometrix of any particular political, scientific, or religious point of view.

22. C: The equation that represents the relationship between the position number, n, and the value of the term, a_n, is $a_n = -3n + 8$. Notice each n is multiplied by –3, with 8 added to that value. Substituting position number 1 for n gives $a_n = -3(1) + 8$, which equals 5. Substitution of the remaining position numbers does not provide a counterexample to this procedure.

23. B: All given sequences have a constant difference of 12. Subtraction of 12 from the starting term, given for Choice B, gives a y-intercept of –9. The equation $123 = 12x - 9$ can thus be written. Solving for x gives $x = 11$; therefore, 123 is indeed the 11th term of this sequence. Manual computation of the 11th term by adding the constant difference of 12 also reveals 123 as the value of the 11th term of this sequence.

24. B: The algebra tiles represent the equation $x + 6 = 15$. Solving for x gives $x = 9$. Note that 6 unit squares are removed from each side of the equation to reveal the remaining 9 unit squares equivalent to the variable x.

25. D: The constant amount Kevin pays is $12.95; this amount represents the y-intercept. The variable amount is represented by the expression $0.07x, where x represents the number of text messages sent and $0.07 represents the constant rate of change or slope. Thus, his total cost can be represented by the equation $y = \$0.07x + \$12.95$.

26. C: Supplementary angles add to 180 degrees. Therefore, the other angle is equal to the difference between 180 degrees and 34 degrees: $180 - 34 = 146$. Thus, the other angle measures 146°.

27. C: The cost per box can be determined by dividing the total cost, c, by the number of boxes, b, included in each total cost. Thus, the cost per box, x, can be determined by dividing c by b. Notice that $15.00 divided by 4 equals a rate of $3.75 per box. A check of the cost per box for the remaining number of boxes confirms a rate of $3.75 per box.

28. A: A triangle with an obtuse angle (an angle greater than 90°) is called an obtuse triangle.

29. C: A square pyramid has 5 faces and 8 edges. There are four triangular faces and a square base.

30. C: A cylinder has two circular bases and a rectangular lateral face.

31. A: The plotted point has an x-value of –2 and a y-value of 5. Thus, the point can be written as an ordered pair in the form $(-2, 5)$.

32. B: A reflection of a figure across the x-axis involves finding the negation (or additive inverse) of the y-value of each coordinate; the x-value stays the same. Negating each y-value gives the vertices $(1, -4)$, $(5, -1)$, and $(5, -6)$.

33. B: Since the intact portion of the cabinet and the missing piece form a 90 degree angle with the wall, the missing piece must have an angle equal to the difference between 90 degrees and 76 degrees. Thus, the newly cut cabinet piece should have an angle measure of 14 degrees.

34. D: A triangular prism has two triangular bases and three rectangular faces.

35. C: The circumference of a circle can be determined by using the formula $C = \pi d$. A radius of 23 cm indicates a diameter of 46 cm, or twice that length. Substitution of 46 cm for d and 3.14 for π gives the following: $C = 3.14 \cdot 46$, which equals 144.44. Thus, the circumference of the circle is approximately 144.44 cm.

36. C: The net approximates a sphere; the joining of all pieces of the net would create a ball.

37. A: Corresponding sides of similar triangles are proportional. Each of the dimensions of the triangle given for Choice A is one-half of the dimensions of Triangle ABC: $18 \div 2 = 9$; $14 \div 2 = 7$, $12 \div 2 = 6$.

38. C: Each side length of the triangle can be rounded to 4 inches. Thus, the estimated perimeter can be written as $4 + 4 + 4$, which equals 12. Therefore, the best estimate for the perimeter of the triangle is 12 in.

39. D: The B in the formula $V = Bh$ represents the area of the triangular base. The formula for the area of a triangle is $\frac{1}{2}bh$, where b represents the length of the triangle's base and h represents the triangle's height.

40. A: The dimensions of the rectangular prism can be rounded to 14 cm, 9 cm, and 12 cm. The volume of a rectangular prism can be determined by finding the product of the length, width, and height. Therefore, the volume is approximately equal to $14 \times 9 \times 12$, or 1,512 cm^3.

41. C: The volume of a cylindrical can be found using the formula $V = \pi r^2 h$, where r represents the radius and h represents the height. Substitution of the given radius and height gives $V = \pi(3.5)^2 \cdot 8$, which is approximately 307.72. Thus, the volume of the can is approximately 307.72 cm^3.

42. C: The volume of a triangular prism can be determined using the formula $V = \frac{1}{2}bhl$, where b represents the length of the base of each triangular face, h represents the height of each triangular face, and l represents the length of the prism. Substitution of the given values into the formula gives $V = \frac{1}{2} \cdot 4 \cdot 7 \cdot 11$, which equals 154. Thus, the volume of the candy box is 154 cubic inches.

43. C: The sample space of independent events is equal to the product of the sample space of each event. The sample space of rolling a die is 6; the sample space of spinning a spinner with four equal sections is 4. Therefore, the overall sample space is equal to 6×4, or 24.

44. B: Flipping a coin three times has the following possible outcomes: HHH, HTH, THT, TTT, HHT, TTH, HTT, and THH. Since there are 8 possible outcomes, the sample space is 8.

45. A: The events are independent since Sarah replaces the first die. The probability of two independent events can be found using the formula $P(A \text{ and } B) = P(A) \cdot P(B)$. The probability of pulling out a blue die is $\frac{2}{12}$. The probability of pulling out a green die is $\frac{4}{12}$. The probability of pulling out a blue die and a green die is $\frac{2}{12} \cdot \frac{4}{12}$, which simplifies to $\frac{1}{18}$.

46. A: A line graph is used to show changes over time. A histogram, line plot, and bar graph compare frequencies of categories.

47. C: The score that has approximately 50% above and 50% below is approximately 500 (517 to be exact). The scores can be manually written by choosing either the lower or upper end of each interval and using the frequency to determine the number of times to record each score, i.e., using the lower end of each interval shows an approximate value of 465 for the median; using the upper end of each interval shows an approximate value of 530 for the median. A score of 500 (and the exact median of 517) is found between 465 and 530.

48. C: The average age indicates the mean. The mean is calculated by summing all ages and dividing by the number of dogs in the sample. Thus, the mean can be calculated by writing $\frac{6+7+2+8+4+1+7+8+3+1+8+2}{12}$, which equals 4.75.

49. B: Whenever the data includes an extreme outlier, such as 39, the median is the best representation of the data. The mean would include that score and heavily skew the data.

50. A: The probability of getting an even number is $\frac{3}{6}$. The probability of getting heads is $\frac{1}{2}$. The probability of both events occurring can be calculated by multiplying the probabilities of the individual events: $\frac{3}{6} \cdot \frac{1}{2}$ equals $\frac{1}{4}$.

51. C: The fractions for Choice C can be compared by either converting all fractions and mixed numbers to decimals or by using a least common denominator. In performing the first suggestion, the fractions as they appear from left to right can be written as −2.875, −2.75, −0.2, 0.125, and 0.4. Negative integers with larger absolute values are less than negative integers with smaller absolute values. The tenths place can be used to compare each of the decimals.

52. C: The fraction $\frac{4}{5}$ can be converted to a decimal by dividing 4 by 5. Doing so gives 0.80, which is equal to 80%.

53. A: The square root of a square is equal to the length of one of the sides, or the number of unit squares comprising a side. For example, a square representing 7 squared will have 7 unit squares on each side; $7^2 = 49$, and 7 is the square root of 49. The square will contain 49 unit squares, with 7 unit squares comprising each side.

54. B: The order of operations states that multiplication and division, as they appear from left to right in the expression, should be completed following the evaluation of exponents. Therefore, after evaluating the squared number, that value should be multiplied by 2.

55. B: In order to determine the number of manuscripts each editor will review, the total number of manuscripts should be divided by the number of editors; $29 \div 8$ can be written as $\frac{29}{8}$, which simplifies to the mixed fraction $3\frac{5}{8}$. Notice that the quotient is 3 with a remainder of 5.

56. D: The counters represent the expression $-12 + 8$, which equals −4. Using the additive inverse property, the eight negative 1 integers and eight positive 1 integers cancel one another, leaving four negative 1 integers, written as −4.

57. C: The following proportion can be used to solve the problem: $\frac{35}{3} = \frac{x}{18}$, where x represents the number of mature trees. Solving for x gives $3x = 630$, which simplifies to $x = 210$.

58. D: The order of operations requires evaluation of the expression inside the parentheses as a first step. Thus, the expression can be re-written as $-8^2 + 8 \times 4 + 7$. Next, the integer with the exponent must be evaluated. Doing so gives $-64 + 8 \times 4 + 7$. The order of operations next requires all multiplications and divisions to be computed as they appear from left to right. Thus, the expression can be written as $-64 + 32 + 7$. Finally, the addition may be computed as it appears from left to right. The expression simplifies to $-32 + 7$, or −25.

59. A: Jason's number can be determined by writing the following expression: $\sqrt{2x - 4}$, where x represents Amy's number. Substitution of 20 for x gives $\sqrt{2(20) - 4}$, which simplifies to $\sqrt{36}$, or 6.

Thus, Jason's number is 6. Jason's number can also be determined by working backwards. If Jason's number is the square root of 4 less than 2 times Amy's number, Amy's number should first be multiplied by 2 with 4 subtracted from that product and the square root taken of the resulting difference.

60. D: The total amount she brought on the trip should be rounded to a reasonable (and compatible) amount; $2,082 can be reasonably rounded to $2,100. $2,100 can easily be divided by 7 days, which gives $300 per day.

61. B: The fraction portion of the mixed number can be converted to a decimal by dividing 3 by 5, which equals 0.6. Therefore, $8\frac{3}{5}$ is equivalent to 8.6.

62. B: In order to determine the total number of cups of sugar used while baking, the product of 5 and $\frac{3}{4}$ should be calculated: $5 \cdot \frac{3}{4} = \frac{15}{4}$, which can be simplified to $3\frac{3}{4}$. Thus, she used $3\frac{3}{4}$ cups in all.

63. A: The following proportion can be used to solve the problem: $\frac{3}{8} = \frac{24}{x}$. Solving for x gives: $3x = 192$, which simplifies to $x = 64$.

64. B: Based on the company's charge per half of an acre, the original charge is equal to 25×4, or $100, since there are 4 half-acres in 2 acres. With the discount of 20%, the following expression can be used to determine the final charge: $x - 0.20x$, where x represents the original charge. Substitution of 100 for x gives $100 - 0.20(100)$, which equals $100 - 20$, or 80. Thus, the company will charge $80.

65. B: The original price was $290,600 ($278,000 + $12,600). In order to determine the percentage of reduction, the following equation can be written: $12,600 = $290,600x$, which simplifies to $x \approx 0.04$, or 4%. Thus, the percentage of reduction was approximately 4%.

66. B: In order to find the unit rate, the cost of the drink should be divided by the number of ounces the drink contains: $\frac{\$1.19}{20} \approx 0.06$. Thus, the cost per ounce is approximately $0.06.

67. D: A proportion can be written to compare the number of hours spent studying for four courses to the number of hours spent studying for five courses. The proportion can be written as: $\frac{25}{4} = \frac{x}{5}$. Solving for x gives $x = 31.25$. Thus, Mel will spend 31.25 hours studying for 5 college courses.

68. B: The volume of a cone can be determined by using the formula $V = \frac{1}{3}\pi r^2 h$. Substitution of the radius and volume into the formula gives $150.72 = \frac{1}{3}\pi(4)^2 h$, which simplifies to $150.72 = \frac{1}{3}\pi 16h$. Division of each side of the equation by $\frac{1}{3}\pi 16$ gives $h = 9$. Thus, the height of the cone is 9 cm.

69. D: The perimeter of a square is equal to 4 times the side length. Therefore, the relationship can be written as $y = 4x$, where y represents the perimeter, and x represents the side length. The graph shown for Choice D shows the line $y = 4x$, where measurable quantities x and y are greater than or equal to zero. The line includes such points as (1, 4), (2, 8), (3, 12), and (4, 16).

70. A: The circumference of a circle is equal to π multiplied by the diameter. This relationship can be written as $C = \pi d$, or $y = \pi x$, where y represents the circumference and x represents the diameter, a measurable quantity which is therefore greater than or equal to zero Some points on the line include (1, 3.14), (2, 6.28), (3, 9.42), and (4, 12.56). The graph shown for Choice A shows the line, $y = \pi x$.

Science

1. C: If two traits are frequently passed on together, the most likely explanation is that these traits correspond to linked genes that are nearby on the same chromosome. In that case, the offspring are likely to inherit both genes from the same parent because the only way they can inherit one of the linked genes from each parent is if, during the process of meiosis, the chromosome happens to split and recombine right between the genes.

2. D: A bacterium is a single-celled organism. All the other organisms mentioned consist of multiple cells. While cells do vary in size, in general, the larger an organism, the more cells it is likely to contain. A mature pine tree is much larger than a housefly or a field mouse and, thus, is very likely to contain more cells.

3. C: Newton's First Law states that an object in motion will tend to remain at motion and an object at rest will tend to remain at rest unless acted on by an outside force. Newton's Second Law states that the larger the force and the smaller the mass, the greater the object's acceleration ($F = ma$). The First Law of Thermodynamics states that energy is not created or destroyed. "For every action, there is an equal and opposite reaction" is Newton's Third Law.

4. B: Hydroelectricity is electricity generated from the power of running water (such as through the generators in Hoover Dam). Solar energy is energy from sunlight, and wind energy is, of course, energy from the wind. All of these are considered renewable energy sources; sun, wind, and the flow of the river are not expended by use and will not run out (in human time frames). Natural gas, however, is expended by use, and takes thousands of years to form. It is therefore not a renewable resource as it is not replenished in human time frames.

5. A: Trace up from five years on the x-axis until the line is then left to see where it intersects the y-axis:

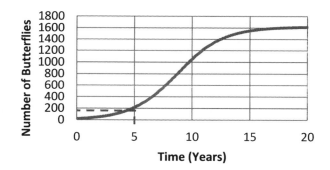

6. C: While the graph shows the butterfly population initially increasing, near the right end of the graph, it seems to be leveling off. This makes sense because any environment has finite resources (food, space, etc.) and can only support a limited number of organisms of any kind.

7. A: *Solubility* is the amount of substance that can be dissolved in a given amount of another substance. It is considered a property of the substance that is dissolved, so there is solubility of sugar in water but not solubility of water in sugar. Because Francis can dissolve more sugar in water than he can salt, the conclusion is that sugar has a higher solubility in water than salt has.

8. C: *Solubility* is a property of a substance; it does not depend on the amount of substance used. While it's true that, with more water, Francis would be able to dissolve more salt (as stated in A), this wouldn't actually change the solubility: If he can dissolve twice as much salt in twice as much water, then the ratio of salt to water—and therefore the solubility—doesn't change.

9. A: While stars are made of plasma and many asteroids are made of iron (though not all—many asteroids are made of rock), comets are mostly ice, with some dust, rock particles, and other impurities mixed in.

10. A: Comets go around the Sun in orbits with fixed periods and, therefore, tend to pass by the Earth at regular intervals. The last two times that 12P/Pons-Brooks passed by the Earth were 70 years apart, so the next time it will pass by the Earth is likely to be 70 years from the last time, or 1954 + 70 = 2024. (In reality, the period of 12P/Pons-Brooks is 70.85 years, but its passages by the Earth aren't exactly 70.85 years apart because they depend on where in its orbit the Earth is when the comet is near the Sun.)

11. B: The *mitochondria* are the organelles (structures inside a cell) that are primarily responsible for generating energy. The *cytoplasm* is the gelatinous fluid that fills the cell; the *nucleus* is the structure at the center of a eukaryotic cell that contains the chromosomes; and a *tissue* is a collection of cells that perform a similar function.

12. D: Heat moves from warmer objects to colder objects. (Cold is merely the absence of heat, so it doesn't make sense to talk about cold being conducted or radiated.) Although all objects do radiate some heat, when an object is in direct contact with another, the heat will move between the objects most efficiently by conduction. Therefore, it's most accurate to say that heat is conducted into the ice cube from the counter and air.

13. D: Matter is not created or destroyed; the water is composed of the same atoms that were in the ice, so the mass must be the same. While it's true that water is denser than ice (which is why ice floats), that doesn't mean the water has more mass than ice; the water will take up a smaller volume, so it can have a higher density but the same mass.

14. B: To find this value, average the three measurements in April for the three different years: 53°F, 54°F, and 58°F. The average is (53 + 54 + 58)/3 = 165/3 = 55°F.

15. C: Whether the student takes measurements in degrees Celsius or Fahrenheit doesn't determine his accuracy; that depends on the accuracy of the instrument with which he's taking the measurements. If he had taken measurements in degrees Celsius instead of Fahrenheit, the numbers for his measurements would have been different, but they still would show the same patterns and be just as useful.

16. D: From the recorded data, it is most likely that the student is in the Southern Hemisphere. The Northern and Southern hemispheres experience the seasons differently. The Northern Hemisphere is in summer in the months of June, July, and August and winter in the months of December, January, and February; the Southern Hemisphere is the other way around. Because the student records average temperatures in January as significantly higher than those in July, it seems that, where he is, it is summer in January and winter in July—as is the case in the Southern Hemisphere.

17. D: A thermometer measures temperature, which is what the student was measuring. An anemometer measures wind speed, a barometer measures pressure, and a multimeter measures various properties of electrical circuits.

18. A: The respiratory system is responsible for gas exchange—taking in oxygen and expelling carbon dioxide. The lungs are where the gas exchange directly takes place as oxygen and carbon dioxide are passed through thin membranes into and out of the blood. The trachea is part of the path through which air enters the lungs. The diaphragm is a muscle that makes the lungs expand to take in air and contract to expel it. All of these play a role in respiration and are part of the respiratory system. The heart, however, is responsible for the circulation of blood and is part of the circulatory system, not the respiratory.

19. C: The nervous system is responsible for gathering information (through the sensory organs, among other means) and for processing that information in the brain. The circulatory system distributes chemicals around the body in the blood; the digestive system takes in food and breaks it down to essential nutrients; and the reproductive system allows for procreation, the generation of offspring.

20. A: Like any object, the mass experiences a downward pull due to gravity. Because the mass is attached to the spring, this pulls downward on the spring as well, stretching it. (Although the mass and the spring do exert gravitational force on each other directly, because their masses are so much smaller than the mass of the Earth, the direct gravitational force they exert on each other is completely insignificant.)

21. C: The problem states that the mass is hanging motionless. In that case, the net force on the mass must be zero. If there were a net force, then there would have to be an acceleration; the mass would have to be moving.

22. B: The g comes after measurements of mass in the table and, therefore, must stand for a unit of mass. In the metric system, g is an abbreviation for grams, a unit of mass, which must be what the g means in the table.

23. B: The phase of the moon is determined by the position of the Sun relative to the moon and the Earth. When the moon and the Sun are on opposite sides of the Earth, the moon is full. A lunar eclipse occurs when the Earth comes directly between the moon and the Sun. In this case, the moon and the Sun must be on opposite sides of the Earth, so the moon must be full. (There isn't a lunar eclipse every time the moon is full because, most of the time, the moon and the Sun aren't directly opposite each other; for a lunar eclipse to occur, the moon, the Earth, and the Sun have to be fairly precisely lined up.)

24. B: Although we breathe oxygen, so we certainly think of it as a major component of the air, it actually makes up only about 21 percent of the atmosphere by volume. The amount of water vapor varies with humidity but is generally around 1 percent. Not counting the water vapor, the atmosphere is about 78 percent nitrogen, 21 percent oxygen, and about 0.9 percent argon; all the other components of the atmosphere make up well under 0.1 percent. (Carbon dioxide is only about 0.04 Percent of the atmosphere.)

25. A: At the edges of tectonic plates, the plates tend to buckle or overlap, letting magma leak through and giving rise to volcanoes. This is the reason why volcanoes are much more common in these areas. (Earthquakes are more frequent in the same areas because the tectonic plates can jerk or shake as they move past each other.)

26. A: The red blood cells carry oxygen; therefore, it is a deficiency in the red blood cells that is most likely to result in too little oxygen reaching the organs. White blood cells destroy pathogens; platelets aid in clotting; and plasma is the fluid in which the blood cells are suspended. Though deficiencies in any of these components could certainly be problematic, it is only the red blood cells that are directly involved in oxygen transport.

27. C: Sea urchins are echinoderms, along with starfish and sea cucumbers. Echinoderms are characterized by radial symmetry, skeletons of calcite plates, and a hydraulic system of locomotion and respiration. Arthropods are animals with jointed exoskeletons, including insects, spiders, and crustaceans (such as crabs and lobsters). Chordates are a group that includes the vertebrates as well as a few lesser-known animals such as sea squirts. Molluscs include snails and slugs as well as cephalopods, such as the octopus.

28. D: One characteristic feature of a plant cell is a large central vacuole, which the cell shown here has. Even without that, though, the cell's other features still show that it's a plant cell. Bacteria don't have nuclei or mitochondria. Animal cells and paramecia (a kind of protozoan) do have nuclei and mitochondria but don't have cell walls or chloroplasts (the organelles that carry out photosynthesis).

29. A: In general, the rougher the material, the greater the friction. Cement is much rougher than polished marble, so it's likely to give rise to greater friction—and rubbing two rough cement blocks together is likely to involve more friction than rubbing one rough cement block with one smooth marble block.

30. B: The buoyant force on an object pushes upward, while gravity pulls downward. If the buoyant force is greater, the net force will be upward, and the object will float. If the force of gravity is greater, the object will sink, and if they are equal, the object will hang suspended in the fluid. (The buoyant force on a submerged object will be greater than the force of gravity on the object whenever the object is less dense than water—for example, if you push a block of pinewood underwater and then let it go, it will float upward because the density of pinewood is less than the density of water.)

31. A: Current is measured in amperes. Joules are a unit of energy, ohms of resistance, and volts of voltage; none of these quantities is the same as current.

32. D: It takes time for the sound to reach the student from the lightning bolt, which is why he sees it before he hears it. Because speed equals distance over time, distance equals speed times time. So if the student knows the speed of sound, he can find the distance by multiplying the speed times the time. (Technically, it also takes time for the light to reach the student from the lightning bolt, but the speed of light is so much larger than the speed of sound that this can be ignored.)

33. D: As mentioned in the answer to question 32, sound travels much more slowly than light, so the light from the lightning bolt will always reach a listener before the sound.

34. C: As an immobile plant, the corpse flower would not need to attract mates, nor would it have to drive away predators, which by definition eat meat (and which, in any case, wouldn't necessarily be driven away by the scent of rotting meat). Nor is there any reason why the smell of rotting meat would inhibit the growth of other plants. However, the main purpose of flowers is to spread their pollen, which is often done by attracting animals to the flower that then unwittingly carry the pollen to other blooms. While many plants use sweet smells to attract insects or bright colors to attract birds, pollination strategies vary, and using the scent of rotten meat to attract flies as pollinators is a viable strategy.

35. B: Both light waves and sound waves have a period and amplitude, occur with many different frequencies, and can be reflected or refracted. (In a light wave, the frequency determines the color; in a sound wave, the pitch. You can see light waves reflected off mirrors; you can sometimes hear reflected sound waves as echoes.) However, sound waves are caused by the physical vibration of a medium and, therefore, require a medium to travel through. Light waves do not require a medium—that's why light from faraway stars can reach us through vast distances across interstellar space.

36. D: Visible light has longer wavelengths than ultraviolet light, and infrared light has longer wavelengths than visible light. However, radio waves have longer wavelengths even than infrared light. (Remember, wavelength is inversely proportional to frequency, so the larger the frequency, the smaller the wavelength. Radio waves have a very long wavelength but a very small frequency.)

37. B: A star is mostly a vast ball of hydrogen gas (or more specifically of plasma, separate electrons, and hydrogen nuclei). Due to the tremendous gravitational pressure because of the star's huge mass, the gas is compressed together to such a high degree that the protons (hydrogen nuclei) contact each other and fuse into helium nuclei, releasing enormous amounts of energy.

38. A: The flat part of the deep ocean floor beyond the continental shelves is the *abyssal plain*. The *mid-ocean ridge* is a rise in the middle of the ocean, while an *oceanic trench* is a deep rift in the ocean floor; both of these occur where two tectonic plates meet and push against each other, buckling either upward or downward. (A *subcontinental plain* is not a real feature of the ocean floor.)

39. A: The phase that a cell spends the most time in is the one it's most likely to be in at any given moment, so she should see more cells in that phase than in any other. The phase in which she sees the most cells is interphase. The order of the phases is irrelevant for determining which one takes the most time.

40. B: In prophase, the chromatin condenses into chromosomes, making the nucleus appear somewhat ropy. In metaphase, the chromosomes line up in a plane called the metaphase plate, or equatorial plane. In anaphase, the chromosomes separate and move toward opposite ends of the cell. Finally, in telophase, the nuclear membranes re-form. (It's also generally during telophase that the cell itself physically divides into two daughter cells, but technically that's not considered part of telophase but a separate though simultaneous process.)

41. D: Bacterial cells are prokaryotic: They do not have nuclei, and they do not undergo mitosis. They do divide into daughter cells, of course, but they do so by a simpler process called binary fission that does not involve all the stages of mitosis.

Social Studies

Civics/Government

1. A: Suffrage refers to the right to vote in political elections. While choices B, C, and D all refer to rights granted in the Bill of Rights, suffrage was a right granted to multiple groups of people by the various amendments.

2. D: The final stage in a bill's journey to law is enactment. After a bill has passed through the preceding steps of the process, the new legislation must still be put into practice and enforced as law.

3. C: The Necessary and Proper Clause grants Congress the power to pass legislation needed for the exercise of its explicit powers. It is sometimes referred to as the Elastic Clause because there is a certain level of flexibility offered by the Constitutional language.

M⊘metrix

4. A: The only way that the Constitution can be altered is through a constitutional amendment. Supreme Court rulings, congressional votes and the presidential veto, while important in the creation of an amendment, cannot directly alter the Constitution of the United States of America.

5. A: Due process refers to the principle that the government must administer justice in a way that protects its citizens from an intrusion on their rights. The wealth and status of an individual should not affect that individual's legal position. Furthermore, due process does not have anything to do with the operational components of government, which are dictated by other portions of the Constitution.

6. D: Franklin D. Roosevelt was the last president to serve more than two terms before a constitutional amendment dictating term limits. Theodore Roosevelt, Calvin Coolidge and Harry S. Truman were each only elected to one full term in office, although each of them finished the term of their predecessors who died while in office.

7. B: The Speaker of the House is the presiding officer of the House of Representatives. The Majority Whip, often viewed as the leader of the majority party in the House of Representatives, is tasked with consolidating their party's voting power. The President pro tempore fulfills the duties of the Vice President in the Senate when he is absent.

8. C: The Emancipation Proclamation was the executive order by Abraham Lincoln that freed all slaves within the Confederate states. The Writ of Habeas Corpus is a legal principle which requires that persons accused of a crime be brought before a court and explained their crime, while the Magna Carta was a legal document signed by the King of England in the 13th Century which codified certain ideals into law.

9. B: A caucus would most likely be used in a primary election with the purpose of selecting a given party's candidate for a general election later on. Primary elections can take place on every level of government, from local elections to the Presidential election.

10. C: The Electoral College is a body of people, representing the members of congress, who cast formal votes to elect the president and vice president. Supreme Court justices are not elected directly by any group of people, they are instead appointed by the sitting President of the United States of America, where after they make rulings from the Supreme Court Building in Washington, D.C.

11. A: Popular sovereignty is the principle that government derives its power from the people. The citizens of the United States of America are able to dictate the direction of the country by electing officials to carry out the people's will.

Geography

1. B: The main concepts through which geography is studied are location, place, interaction between humans and their environment, movement and region. This lengthy list of core concepts speaks to the array of areas studied by geography, encompassing subjects as seemingly distinct as culture and sources of water.

2. B: The Middle East is a region. A region is an area with definable characteristics that does not always have fixed boundaries. This definition of region is distinct from countries, cities, and continents, all of which do have fixed boundaries.

3. A: Israel shares a border with Egypt. The northeastern African nation of Egypt also shares a border with the Gaza Strip and the nations of Libya and Sudan. The nations of Turkey, Iran, and India are situated to the north, northeast, and east of Egypt, respectively.

4. D: Egypt shares a common culture with Iran. While Egypt does not share a border with Iran, the two nations share a common Arab culture that is distinct from the cultures of Israel, India, and Turkey.

5. A: Civilizations located on fertile soil tend to cultivate and farm, while civilizations close to bodies of water learn to fish is an example of adaptation. Humans adapt to their environment instead of allowing their environment to be a limitation.

6. D: Isolationism intrinsically impedes cultural diffusion by restricting the amount of contact with other nations. European colonialism, immigration, and (most recently) the Internet are all means by which cultural diffusion has taken or may take place.

7. D: Drought is the correct answer. Because of the lack of rain, fewer plants grow; because of this, the wind is able to move soil more easily, leaving the landscape barren. Heat, while not helpful, does not on its own contribute to the desertification of the Saharan region.

8. C: Erosion is the gradual process of destruction or diminution by wind, water, or other natural means. While flooding or tectonic shifts may cause destruction or diminution, those occur by sudden means as opposed to a gradual process.

9. B: A historical map is best suited for depicting battles and military campaigns. Historical maps depict events, troop movements, historical locations and other features necessary for understanding battlefields. Alternatively, political maps show man-made features such as boundaries, roads, and cities, while physical maps show natural features such as rivers, deserts, and valleys.

10. C: A map legend explains the colors, lines, and other symbols on a map. Map projections deal with representing a three-dimensional object on a two-dimensional plane, scale deals with the size of the area that is represented and, lastly, the compass rose orients the direction of the map.

History

1. B: Zebulon Pike's expeditions included the Arkansas River, the Rocky Mountains, and the Rio Grande. Lewis and Clark were also explorers whose expedition focused on crossing the continental divide en route to the Pacific Ocean. While contemporaries with the explorers, neither Henry Clay, a 19th century American politician, nor Toussaint L'Overture, leader of the revolution in Haiti, explored the areas that Pike explored.

2. C: The War of 1812 began as a result of British interference with trade in the United States. Independence was gained in 1783 at the end of the Revolutionary War; it was at this point that the British surrendered control of their colonies in what is now the United States of America. The Revolutionary War also secured religious freedom for the former colonists.

3. B: The development of the factory system was a major result of the Industrial Revolution. By its very nature, the Industrial Revolution saw an increase in large-scale manufacturing and a move away from rural areas. Another result of the Industrial Revolution is that more natural commodities were being produced in America than ever before.

4. D: The Civil Rights Act of 1866 granted citizenship to all people of the United States except Native Americans. While this citizenship was not equal to what Americans know today, it was a step toward equality for immigrants in the United States.

5. A: Andrew Johnson insisting that the new state governments in the South ratify the 13th Amendment abolishing slavery was not a reason for his impeachment, as the amendment was ratified prior to his taking office. Johnson's presidency was the first of the post-Civil War United States, and tensions were still at a boiling point.

6. C: Slaves starting an Underground Railroad was not a reason for the South's secession from the Union in 1861. The North and South had very different beliefs regarding how the country should be run; the election of Abraham Lincoln and the views he represented served as a catalyst for the South's secession.

7. B: Maryland did not secede from the Union. South Carolina was the first state to secede on December 20, 1860, followed by Mississippi, Florida, Alabama, Georgia, Louisiana, Texas, Virginia, Arkansas, North Carolina and Tennessee.

8. D: Southern animosity toward so-called "carpetbaggers" is multifaceted, with reasons ranging from exploitation to corruption. There are instances of people traveling from the North to take advantage of financial opportunities in the devastated South, convincing the newly-freed slaves to run for political office, and taking advantage of newly impoverished plantation owners to gain land and political power. The answer is all of the above.

9. D: The Battle of Antietam was fought during the Civil War. The Battles of Bunker Hill and Yorktown were fought during the Revolutionary War, while the Battle of the Bulge took place in the 20th century during World War II.

10. C: African-American men were the first minority group to gain the right of suffrage. It was not until 1920 that the 19th Amendment granted women the right to vote and 1948 that restrictions on Native American voting were lifted.

11. A: Benjamin Franklin never served as President of the United States. Hayes, Arthur, and Harrison all served as one-term republican presidents at the end of the 19th century.

Economics

1. C: The United States of America operates under a capitalist economic model. Barter systems are more primitive in nature, exchanging goods without the use of currency. Capitalism prescribes private ownership of wealth, whereas socialism and communism prescribe collective and government ownership of wealth, respectively.

2. D: Water, time, and raw materials are all examples of commodities. They are useful and valuable things that can be bought or sold in their original form. Conversely, common goods and products are commodities that have been tooled to serve a specific purpose. Liquid assets refer to wealth that can easily be used as a currency, such as cash.

3. B: Inflation is defined by a fall in the value of a currency coupled with an overall increase in prices. Inflation may lead to an economic crisis, recession, or stock market collapse, but does not necessarily lead to such an end.

4. C: A gross domestic product (GDP) is the dollar value of all goods and services that a country produces in a year. While this may be an indication of a country's quality of life or amount of natural resources, there is not a guaranteed correlation.

5. A: The concept of supply and demand dictates that a highly desired product causes prices to rise. According to this economic principle, the more consumers want a product, the amount that they are willing to pay also rises, and thus it may be concluded that prices would not remain stagnant or fluctuate inconsistently.

6. A: The federal government providing purchasing incentives for electric car buyers is an example of a subsidy. Government-prompted incentives would not necessarily create a change in demand. A mandate is another word for an order while a stipulation is another word for a condition of an agreement.

7. D: An interest rate is a percentage paid for the ability to borrow money over a specified amount of time. Individuals may pay interest for the privilege of using a credit card or may be paid interest by banks so that they may use investor's capitol for their own purposes.

8. B: A copyright is a means by which companies can protect ideas and products from competitors. This is a common tool for entrepreneurs and corporations that develop new technologies.

9. A: Commerce is the activity of buying and selling. Commerce is the means by which business operates and generally involves the transfer of goods and services in and between economies.

Vocabulary

1. B: limousine driver

2. A: not important

3. C: long speech

4. C: poisonous

5. D: take away

6. A: hard to please

7. C: expensive

8. D: came up with

9. A: friendly

10. D: a person who prefers to be alone

11. B: moving to a new place when the season changes

12. D: things that makes something difficult

13. B: a huge amount

14. B: harmful to others

15. C: very loud

16. D: completely wet

17. A: unworthy of respect

18. B: skillful movement

19. D: a great disturbance

20. A: strong

21. C: impossible to disprove

22. D: extremely slow

23. C: inside

24. A: seized unlawfully

25. A: unusual

26. C: someone whose behavior is uncivilized

27. B: go before

28. C: impossible to solve

29. A: able to be heard

30. B: hide

31. D: disorganized

32. B: two things that should match up but don't

33. A: energetic enthusiasm

34. B: unexplained sadness

35. C: adjust

36. D: annoying

37. D: unavoidable

38. A: calm

39. B: changed

40. B: low in quality

41. C: clothing

Spelling

1. *ballut* – this should be *ballot*

2. overwelming – this should be overwhelming

3. accumpany – this should be accompany

4. vaxination – this should be vaccination

5. shepard – this should be shepherd

6. suvenere – this should be souvenir

7. *moralle* – this should be *morale*

8. amfibian – this should be amphibian

9. *scolar* – this should be *scholar*

10. newmonia – this should be pneumonia

11. *rithum* – this should be *rhythm*

12. peediatrician – this should be pediatrician

13. monitter – this should be monitor

14. confiskate – this should be confiscate

15. imobilize – this should be immobilize

16. solutary – this should be solitary

17. merchendice – this should be merchandise

18. regurjitate – this should be regurgitate

19. *endulge-* this should be *indulge*

20. *indeuce* – this should be *induce*

21. NO MISTAKES

22. dalinquent – this should be delinquent

23. counterfit – this should be counterfeit

24. clientell – this should be clientele

25. *pleeted* – this should be *pleated*

26. embaras – this should be embarrass

27. decafinated – this should be decaffeinated

28. cullprit – this should be culprit

29. ocasional – this should be occasional

30. serennity – this should be serenity

31. labaratory – this should be laboratory

32. ajerned – this should be adjourned

33. recuring – this should be recurring

34. *boyant* – this should be *buoyant*

Capitalization

1. B: We went shopping for clothes at the Mall.

Correct: We went shopping for clothes at the mall.

2. A: I know all the words to the star-spangled banner.

Correct: I know all the words to the Star-Spangled Banner.

3. C: Francis Scott Key wrote the lyrics to the National Anthem.

Correct: Francis Scott Key wrote the lyrics to the national anthem.

4. A: My cousin will start his Military Career at Fort Leonard Wood.

Correct: My cousin will start his military career at Fort Leonard Wood.

5. A: I think he's got a good shot at being named rookie of the year.

Correct: I think he's got a good shot at being named Rookie of the Year.

6. B: He had memorized the Multiplication Table by age 4.

Correct: He had memorized the multiplication table by age 4.

7. C: Our family goes to six flags over Texas every summer.

Correct: Our family goes to Six Flags Over Texas every summer.

8. A: There are 66 books in the bible.

Correct: There are 66 books in the Bible.

9. C: Man, it sounds like there's a War going on in the gym!

Correct: Man, it sounds like there's a war going on in the gym!

10. C: The Russian Language is one of the most difficult to learn.

Correct: The Russian language is one of the most difficult to learn.

11. B: We called the number on the flyer on the Bulletin Board at Kroger.

Correct: We called the number on the flyer on the bulletin board at Kroger.

12. A: Many people think Television was invented in 1947, but that is incorrect.

Correct: Many people think television was invented in 1947, but that is incorrect.

13. C: My Birthday is July 17th.

Correct: My birthday is July 17th.

14. B: I named them after the flintstones characters.

Correct: I named them after the Flintstones characters.

15. C: We need to leave no later than Noon.

Correct: We need to leave no later than noon.

16. C: At the zoo I saw Lions, Bears, and Jaguars.

Correct: At the zoo I saw lions, bears, and jaguars.

17. NO MISTAKES

18. B: This is the First Amendment the city council has made to the zoning law in over 20 years.

Correct: This is the first amendment the city council has made to the zoning law in over 20 years.

19. A: There are three breeds of Ducks at the park: Muscovy, Ancona, and Pekin.

Correct: There are three breeds of ducks at the park: Muscovy, Ancona, and Pekin.

20. B: I didn't care for most of the Art Pieces on display in that museum.

Correct: I didn't care for most of the art pieces on display in that museum.

21. B: Have you made any resolutions for the coming New Year?

Correct: Have you made any resolutions for the coming new year?

22. A: My mom is a republican, but my dad is a democrat.

Correct: My mom is a Republican, but my dad is a Democrat.

23. B: If you see something suspicious, call the Police at once.

Correct: If you see something suspicious, call the police at once.

24. C: I hope my Pumpkin Pie takes 1st Prize at this year's Pumpkin Festival.

Correct: I hope my pumpkin pie takes 1st Prize at this year's Pumpkin Festival.

25. B: I like reading everything I can find about the nba or the nfl.

Correct: I like reading everything I can find about the NBA or the NFL.

26. A: Dr. Seuss wasn't a real Doctor.

Correct: Dr. Seuss wasn't a real doctor.

27. C: Professor, do you think we'll ever be able to go backward in Time?

Correct: Professor, do you think we'll ever be able to go backward in Time?

Punctuation

1. B: Mom and Dad are tired (we're heading home).

Should be: *Mom and Dad are tired, so we're heading home.*

2. B: All's well, that ends well.

Should be: *All's well that ends well.*

3. C: Zach and Sally you will be lab partners.

Should be: *Zach and Sally, you will be lab partners.*

4. A: Dad said – to ask you to make a grocery list.

Should be: *Dad said to ask you to make a grocery list.*

5. A: For whom, does the bell toll?

Should be: *For whom does the bell toll?*

6. C: Mrs. Garcia said there will be a test (on Friday).

Should be: *Mrs. Garcia said there will be a test on Friday.*

7. C: My kitten is "six months old" today.

Should be: *My kitten is six months old today.*

8. B: These are the team captains; Jake, Shelley, Frannie, and Tom.

Should be: *These are the team captains: Jake, Shelley, Frannie, and Tom.*

9. B: The Smith's oldest son just graduated from law school.

Should be: *The Smiths' oldest son just graduated from law school.*

10. A: The class motto is "Striving for Excellence".

Should be: *The class motto is "Striving for Excellence."*

11. C: The teacher, asked Mary who had been interrupting, to stay after class.

Should be: *The teacher asked Mary, who had been interrupting, to stay after class.*

12. A: If you're going to do something why not do it right the first time?

Should be: *If you're going to do something, why not do it right the first time?*

13. A: My neighbor is a truck driver who's on the road a lot so I rarely see him.

Should be: *My neighbor is a truck driver who's on the road a lot, so I rarely see him.*

14. NO MISTAKES

15. A: The clown smiled waved and took a deep bow.

Should be: *The clown smiled, waved, and took a deep bow.*

16. NO MISTAKES

17. B: The other team scored; six runs in the ninth inning.

Should be: *The other team scored; six runs in the ninth inning.*

18. B: Kids, study hard in school, because the future will be here, before you know it.

Should be: *Kids, study hard in school, because the future will be here before you know it.*

19. A: Be that as it may we should delay the vote until all members are present.

Should be: *Be that as it may, we should delay the vote until all members are present.*

20. B: Did Jack really say "I can't make it tonight?"

Should be: *Did Jack really say "I can't make it tonight"?*

21. C: Actually I find playing with wooden blocks to be a great way of relaxing.

Should be: *Actually, I find playing with wooden blocks to be a great way of relaxing.*

22. A: Too many people take the 'lesser of two evils' approach to voting.

Should be: *Too many people take the "lesser of two evils" approach to voting.*

23. B: Am I dreaming or has school really been canceled due to snow?

Should be: *Am I dreaming, or has school really been canceled due to snow?*

24. A: The quick brown, fox jumps over the lazy dog.

Should be: *The quick brown fox jumps over the lazy dog.*

25. C: Mom said and this is an exact quote, "No way, Jose!"

Should be: *Mom said – and this is an exact quote – "No way, Jose!"*

26. A: Did you ever, see such a thing?

Should be: *Did you ever see such a thing?*

27. C: Easy come easy go.

Should be: *Easy come, easy go.*

How to Overcome Test Anxiety

Just the thought of taking a test is enough to make most people a little nervous. A test is an important event that can have a long-term impact on your future, so it's important to take it seriously and it's natural to feel anxious about performing well. But just because anxiety is normal, that doesn't mean that it's helpful in test taking, or that you should simply accept it as part of your life. Anxiety can have a variety of effects. These effects can be mild, like making you feel slightly nervous, or severe, like blocking your ability to focus or remember even a simple detail.

If you experience test anxiety—whether severe or mild—it's important to know how to beat it. To discover this, first you need to understand what causes test anxiety.

Causes of Test Anxiety

While we often think of anxiety as an uncontrollable emotional state, it can actually be caused by simple, practical things. One of the most common causes of test anxiety is that a person does not feel adequately prepared for their test. This feeling can be the result of many different issues such as poor study habits or lack of organization, but the most common culprit is time management. Starting to study too late, failing to organize your study time to cover all of the material, or being distracted while you study will mean that you're not well prepared for the test. This may lead to cramming the night before, which will cause you to be physically and mentally exhausted for the test. Poor time management also contributes to feelings of stress, fear, and hopelessness as you realize you are not well prepared but don't know what to do about it.

Other times, test anxiety is not related to your preparation for the test but comes from unresolved fear. This may be a past failure on a test, or poor performance on tests in general. It may come from comparing yourself to others who seem to be performing better or from the stress of living up to expectations. Anxiety may be driven by fears of the future—how failure on this test would affect your educational and career goals. These fears are often completely irrational, but they can still negatively impact your test performance.

> **Review Video: <u>3 Reasons You Have Test Anxiety</u>**
> Visit mometrix.com/academy and enter code: 428468

119

Elements of Test Anxiety

As mentioned earlier, test anxiety is considered to be an emotional state, but it has physical and mental components as well. Sometimes you may not even realize that you are suffering from test anxiety until you notice the physical symptoms. These can include trembling hands, rapid heartbeat, sweating, nausea, and tense muscles. Extreme anxiety may lead to fainting or vomiting. Obviously, any of these symptoms can have a negative impact on testing. It is important to recognize them as soon as they begin to occur so that you can address the problem before it damages your performance.

> **Review Video: 3 Ways to Tell You Have Test Anxiety**
> Visit mometrix.com/academy and enter code: 927847

The mental components of test anxiety include trouble focusing and inability to remember learned information. During a test, your mind is on high alert, which can help you recall information and stay focused for an extended period of time. However, anxiety interferes with your mind's natural processes, causing you to blank out, even on the questions you know well. The strain of testing during anxiety makes it difficult to stay focused, especially on a test that may take several hours. Extreme anxiety can take a huge mental toll, making it difficult not only to recall test information but even to understand the test questions or pull your thoughts together.

> **Review Video: How Test Anxiety Affects Memory**
> Visit mometrix.com/academy and enter code: 609003

Effects of Test Anxiety

Test anxiety is like a disease—if left untreated, it will get progressively worse. Anxiety leads to poor performance, and this reinforces the feelings of fear and failure, which in turn lead to poor performances on subsequent tests. It can grow from a mild nervousness to a crippling condition. If allowed to progress, test anxiety can have a big impact on your schooling, and consequently on your future.

Test anxiety can spread to other parts of your life. Anxiety on tests can become anxiety in any stressful situation, and blanking on a test can turn into panicking in a job situation. But fortunately, you don't have to let anxiety rule your testing and determine your grades. There are a number of relatively simple steps you can take to move past anxiety and function normally on a test and in the rest of life.

> **Review Video: How Test Anxiety Impacts Your Grades**
> Visit mometrix.com/academy and enter code: 939819

Physical Steps for Beating Test Anxiety

While test anxiety is a serious problem, the good news is that it can be overcome. It doesn't have to control your ability to think and remember information. While it may take time, you can begin taking steps today to beat anxiety.

Just as your first hint that you may be struggling with anxiety comes from the physical symptoms, the first step to treating it is also physical. Rest is crucial for having a clear, strong mind. If you are tired, it is much easier to give in to anxiety. But if you establish good sleep habits, your body and mind will be ready to perform optimally, without the strain of exhaustion. Additionally, sleeping well helps you to retain information better, so you're more likely to recall the answers when you see the test questions.

Getting good sleep means more than going to bed on time. It's important to allow your brain time to relax. Take study breaks from time to time so it doesn't get overworked, and don't study right before bed. Take time to rest your mind before trying to rest your body, or you may find it difficult to fall asleep.

> **Review Video: The Importance of Sleep for Your Brain**
> Visit mometrix.com/academy and enter code: 319338

Along with sleep, other aspects of physical health are important in preparing for a test. Good nutrition is vital for good brain function. Sugary foods and drinks may give a burst of energy but this burst is followed by a crash, both physically and emotionally. Instead, fuel your body with protein and vitamin-rich foods.

Also, drink plenty of water. Dehydration can lead to headaches and exhaustion, especially if your brain is already under stress from the rigors of the test. Particularly if your test is a long one, drink water during the breaks. And if possible, take an energy-boosting snack to eat between sections.

> **Review Video: How Diet Can Affect your Mood**
> Visit mometrix.com/academy and enter code: 624317

Along with sleep and diet, a third important part of physical health is exercise. Maintaining a steady workout schedule is helpful, but even taking 5-minute study breaks to walk can help get your blood pumping faster and clear your head. Exercise also releases endorphins, which contribute to a positive feeling and can help combat test anxiety.

When you nurture your physical health, you are also contributing to your mental health. If your body is healthy, your mind is much more likely to be healthy as well. So take time to rest, nourish your body with healthy food and water, and get moving as much as possible. Taking these physical steps will make you stronger and more able to take the mental steps necessary to overcome test anxiety.

Mental Steps for Beating Test Anxiety

Working on the mental side of test anxiety can be more challenging, but as with the physical side, there are clear steps you can take to overcome it. As mentioned earlier, test anxiety often stems from lack of preparation, so the obvious solution is to prepare for the test. Effective studying may be the most important weapon you have for beating test anxiety, but you can and should employ several other mental tools to combat fear.

First, boost your confidence by reminding yourself of past success—tests or projects that you aced. If you're putting as much effort into preparing for this test as you did for those, there's no reason you should expect to fail here. Work hard to prepare; then trust your preparation.

Second, surround yourself with encouraging people. It can be helpful to find a study group, but be sure that the people you're around will encourage a positive attitude. If you spend time with others who are anxious or cynical, this will only contribute to your own anxiety. Look for others who are motivated to study hard from a desire to succeed, not from a fear of failure.

Third, reward yourself. A test is physically and mentally tiring, even without anxiety, and it can be helpful to have something to look forward to. Plan an activity following the test, regardless of the outcome, such as going to a movie or getting ice cream.

When you are taking the test, if you find yourself beginning to feel anxious, remind yourself that you know the material. Visualize successfully completing the test. Then take a few deep, relaxing breaths and return to it. Work through the questions carefully but with confidence, knowing that you are capable of succeeding.

Developing a healthy mental approach to test taking will also aid in other areas of life. Test anxiety affects more than just the actual test—it can be damaging to your mental health and even contribute to depression. It's important to beat test anxiety before it becomes a problem for more than testing.

> **Review Video: Test Anxiety and Depression**
> Visit mometrix.com/academy and enter code: 904704

Study Strategy

Being prepared for the test is necessary to combat anxiety, but what does being prepared look like? You may study for hours on end and still not feel prepared. What you need is a strategy for test prep. The next few pages outline our recommended steps to help you plan out and conquer the challenge of preparation.

STEP 1: SCOPE OUT THE TEST

Learn everything you can about the format (multiple choice, essay, etc.) and what will be on the test. Gather any study materials, course outlines, or sample exams that may be available. Not only will this help you to prepare, but knowing what to expect can help to alleviate test anxiety.

STEP 2: MAP OUT THE MATERIAL

Look through the textbook or study guide and make note of how many chapters or sections it has. Then divide these over the time you have. For example, if a book has 15 chapters and you have five days to study, you need to cover three chapters each day. Even better, if you have the time, leave an extra day at the end for overall review after you have gone through the material in depth.

If time is limited, you may need to prioritize the material. Look through it and make note of which sections you think you already have a good grasp on, and which need review. While you are studying, skim quickly through the familiar sections and take more time on the challenging parts. Write out your plan so you don't get lost as you go. Having a written plan also helps you feel more in control of the study, so anxiety is less likely to arise from feeling overwhelmed at the amount to cover.

STEP 3: GATHER YOUR TOOLS

Decide what study method works best for you. Do you prefer to highlight in the book as you study and then go back over the highlighted portions? Or do you type out notes of the important information? Or is it helpful to make flashcards that you can carry with you? Assemble the pens, index cards, highlighters, post-it notes, and any other materials you may need so you won't be distracted by getting up to find things while you study.

If you're having a hard time retaining the information or organizing your notes, experiment with different methods. For example, try color-coding by subject with colored pens, highlighters, or post-it notes. If you learn better by hearing, try recording yourself reading your notes so you can listen while in the car, working out, or simply sitting at your desk. Ask a friend to quiz you from your flashcards, or try teaching someone the material to solidify it in your mind.

STEP 4: CREATE YOUR ENVIRONMENT

It's important to avoid distractions while you study. This includes both the obvious distractions like visitors and the subtle distractions like an uncomfortable chair (or a too-comfortable couch that makes you want to fall asleep). Set up the best study environment possible: good lighting and a comfortable work area. If background music helps you focus, you may want to turn it on, but otherwise keep the room quiet. If you are using a computer to take notes, be sure you don't have any other windows open, especially applications like social media, games, or anything else that could distract you. Silence your phone and turn off notifications. Be sure to keep water close by so you stay hydrated while you study (but avoid unhealthy drinks and snacks).

Also, take into account the best time of day to study. Are you freshest first thing in the morning? Try to set aside some time then to work through the material. Is your mind clearer in the afternoon or evening? Schedule your study session then. Another method is to study at the same time of day that you will take the test, so that your brain gets used to working on the material at that time and will be ready to focus at test time.

STEP 5: STUDY!

Once you have done all the study preparation, it's time to settle into the actual studying. Sit down, take a few moments to settle your mind so you can focus, and begin to follow your study plan. Don't give in to distractions or let yourself procrastinate. This is your time to prepare so you'll be ready to fearlessly approach the test. Make the most of the time and stay focused.

Of course, you don't want to burn out. If you study too long you may find that you're not retaining the information very well. Take regular study breaks. For example, taking five minutes out of every hour to walk briskly, breathing deeply and swinging your arms, can help your mind stay fresh.

As you get to the end of each chapter or section, it's a good idea to do a quick review. Remind yourself of what you learned and work on any difficult parts. When you feel that you've mastered the material, move on to the next part. At the end of your study session, briefly skim through your notes again.

But while review is helpful, cramming last minute is NOT. If at all possible, work ahead so that you won't need to fit all your study into the last day. Cramming overloads your brain with more information than it can process and retain, and your tired mind may struggle to recall even previously learned information when it is overwhelmed with last-minute study. Also, the urgent nature of cramming and the stress placed on your brain contribute to anxiety. You'll be more likely to go to the test feeling unprepared and having trouble thinking clearly.

So don't cram, and don't stay up late before the test, even just to review your notes at a leisurely pace. Your brain needs rest more than it needs to go over the information again. In fact, plan to finish your studies by noon or early afternoon the day before the test. Give your brain the rest of the day to relax or focus on other things, and get a good night's sleep. Then you will be fresh for the test and better able to recall what you've studied.

STEP 6: TAKE A PRACTICE TEST

Many courses offer sample tests, either online or in the study materials. This is an excellent resource to check whether you have mastered the material, as well as to prepare for the test format and environment.

Check the test format ahead of time: the number of questions, the type (multiple choice, free response, etc.), and the time limit. Then create a plan for working through them. For example, if you have 30 minutes to take a 60-question test, your limit is 30 seconds per question. Spend less time on the questions you know well so that you can take more time on the difficult ones.

If you have time to take several practice tests, take the first one open book, with no time limit. Work through the questions at your own pace and make sure you fully understand them. Gradually work up to taking a test under test conditions: sit at a desk with all study materials put away and set a timer. Pace yourself to make sure you finish the test with time to spare and go back to check your answers if you have time.

After each test, check your answers. On the questions you missed, be sure you understand why you missed them. Did you misread the question (tests can use tricky wording)? Did you forget the information? Or was it something you hadn't learned? Go back and study any shaky areas that the practice tests reveal.

Taking these tests not only helps with your grade, but also aids in combating test anxiety. If you're already used to the test conditions, you're less likely to worry about it, and working through tests until you're scoring well gives you a confidence boost. Go through the practice tests until you feel comfortable, and then you can go into the test knowing that you're ready for it.

Test Tips

On test day, you should be confident, knowing that you've prepared well and are ready to answer the questions. But aside from preparation, there are several test day strategies you can employ to maximize your performance.

First, as stated before, get a good night's sleep the night before the test (and for several nights before that, if possible). Go into the test with a fresh, alert mind rather than staying up late to study.

Try not to change too much about your normal routine on the day of the test. It's important to eat a nutritious breakfast, but if you normally don't eat breakfast at all, consider eating just a protein bar. If you're a coffee drinker, go ahead and have your normal coffee. Just make sure you time it so that the caffeine doesn't wear off right in the middle of your test. Avoid sugary beverages, and drink enough water to stay hydrated but not so much that you need a restroom break 10 minutes into the test. If your test isn't first thing in the morning, consider going for a walk or doing a light workout before the test to get your blood flowing.

Allow yourself enough time to get ready, and leave for the test with plenty of time to spare so you won't have the anxiety of scrambling to arrive in time. Another reason to be early is to select a good seat. It's helpful to sit away from doors and windows, which can be distracting. Find a good seat, get out your supplies, and settle your mind before the test begins.

When the test begins, start by going over the instructions carefully, even if you already know what to expect. Make sure you avoid any careless mistakes by following the directions.

Then begin working through the questions, pacing yourself as you've practiced. If you're not sure on an answer, don't spend too much time on it, and don't let it shake your confidence. Either skip it and come back later, or eliminate as many wrong answers as possible and guess among the remaining ones. Don't dwell on these questions as you continue—put them out of your mind and focus on what lies ahead.

Be sure to read all of the answer choices, even if you're sure the first one is the right answer. Sometimes you'll find a better one if you keep reading. But don't second-guess yourself if you do immediately know the answer. Your gut instinct is usually right. Don't let test anxiety rob you of the information you know.

If you have time at the end of the test (and if the test format allows), go back and review your answers. Be cautious about changing any, since your first instinct tends to be correct, but make sure you didn't misread any of the questions or accidentally mark the wrong answer choice. Look over any you skipped and make an educated guess.

At the end, leave the test feeling confident. You've done your best, so don't waste time worrying about your performance or wishing you could change anything. Instead, celebrate the successful

completion of this test. And finally, use this test to learn how to deal with anxiety even better next time.

Important Qualification

Not all anxiety is created equal. If your test anxiety is causing major issues in your life beyond the classroom or testing center, or if you are experiencing troubling physical symptoms related to your anxiety, it may be a sign of a serious physiological or psychological condition. If this sounds like your situation, we strongly encourage you to seek professional help.

How to Overcome Your Fear of Math

Not again. You're sitting in math class, look down at your test, and immediately start to panic. Your stomach is in knots, your heart is racing, and you break out in a cold sweat. You're staring at the paper, but everything looks like it's written in a foreign language. Even though you studied, you're blanking out on how to begin solving these problems.

Does this sound familiar? If so, then you're not alone! You may be like millions of other people who experience math anxiety. Anxiety about performing well in math is a common experience for students of all ages. In this article, we'll discuss what math anxiety is, common misconceptions about learning math, and tips and strategies for overcoming math anxiety.

What Is Math Anxiety?

Psychologist Mark H. Ashcraft explains math anxiety as a feeling of tension, apprehension, or fear that interferes with math performance. Having math anxiety negatively impacts people's beliefs about themselves and what they can achieve. It hinders achievement within the math classroom and affects the successful application of mathematics in the real world.

SYMPTOMS AND SIGNS OF MATH ANXIETY

To overcome math anxiety, you must recognize its symptoms. Becoming aware of the signs of math anxiety is the first step in addressing and resolving these fears.

NEGATIVE SELF-TALK

If you have math anxiety, you've most likely said at least one of these statements to yourself:

- "I hate math."
- "I'm not good at math."
- "I'm not a math person."

The way we speak to ourselves and think about ourselves matters. Our thoughts become our words, our words become our actions, and our actions become our habits. Thinking negatively about math creates a self-fulfilling prophecy. In other words, if you take an idea as a fact, then it will come true because your behaviors will align to match it.

AVOIDANCE

Some people who are fearful or anxious about math will tend to avoid it altogether. Avoidance can manifest in the following ways:

- Lack of engagement with math content
- Not completing homework and other assignments
- Not asking for help when needed
- Skipping class
- Avoiding math-related courses and activities

Avoidance is one of the most harmful impacts of math anxiety. If you steer clear of math at all costs, then you can't set yourself up for the success you deserve.

LACK OF MOTIVATION

Students with math anxiety may experience a lack of motivation. They may struggle to find the incentive to get engaged with what they view as a frightening subject. These students are often overwhelmed, making it difficult for them to complete or even start math assignments.

PROCRASTINATION

Another symptom of math anxiety is procrastination. Students may voluntarily delay or postpone their classwork and assignments, even if they know there will be a negative consequence for doing so. Additionally, they may choose to wait until the last minute to start projects and homework, even when they know they need more time to put forth their best effort.

PHYSIOLOGICAL REACTIONS

Many people with a fear of math experience physiological side effects. These may include an increase in heart rate, sweatiness, shakiness, nausea, and irregular breathing. These symptoms make it difficult to focus on the math content, causing the student even more stress and fear.

STRONG EMOTIONAL RESPONSES

Math anxiety also affects people on an emotional level. Responding to math content with strong emotions such as panic, anger, or despair can be a sign of math anxiety.

LOW TEST SCORES AND PERFORMANCE

Low achievement can be both a symptom and a cause of math anxiety. When someone does not take the steps needed to perform well on tests and assessments, they are less likely to pass. The more they perform poorly, the more they accept this poor performance as a fact that can't be changed.

FEELING ALONE

People who experience math anxiety feel like they are the only ones struggling, even if the math they are working on is challenging to many people. Feeling isolated in what they perceive as failure can trigger tension or nervousness.

FEELING OF PERMANENCY

Math anxiety can feel very permanent. You may assume that you are naturally bad at math and always will be. Viewing math as a natural ability rather than a skill that can be learned causes people to believe that nothing will help them improve. They take their current math abilities as fact and assume that they can't be changed. As a result, they give up, stop trying to improve, and avoid engaging with math altogether.

LACK OF CONFIDENCE

People with low self-confidence in math tend to feel awkward and incompetent when asked to solve a math problem. They don't feel comfortable taking chances or risks when problem-solving because they second-guess themselves and assume they are incorrect. They don't trust in their ability to learn the content and solve problems correctly.

PANIC

A general sense of unexplained panic is also a sign of math anxiety. You may feel a sudden sense of fear that triggers physical reactions, even when there is no apparent reason for such a response.

CAUSES OF MATH ANXIETY

Math anxiety can start at a young age and may have one or more underlying causes. Common causes of math anxiety include the following:

THE ATTITUDE OF PARENTS OR GUARDIANS

Parents often put pressure on their children to perform well in school. Although their intentions are usually good, this pressure can lead to anxiety, especially if the student is struggling with a subject or class.

Perhaps your parents or others in your life hold negative predispositions about math based on their own experiences. For instance, if your mother once claimed she was not good at math, then you might have incorrectly interpreted this as a predisposed trait that was passed down to you.

TEACHER INFLUENCE

Students often pick up on their teachers' attitudes about the content being taught. If a teacher is happy and excited about math, students are more likely to mirror these emotions. However, if a teacher lacks enthusiasm or genuine interest, then students are more inclined to disengage.

Teachers have a responsibility to cultivate a welcoming classroom culture that is accepting of mistakes. When teachers blame students for not understanding a concept, they create a hostile classroom environment where mistakes are not tolerated. This tension increases student stress and anxiety, creating conditions that are not conducive to inquiry and learning. Instead, when teachers normalize mistakes as a natural part of the problem-solving process, they give their students the freedom to explore and grapple with the math content. In such an environment, students feel comfortable taking chances because they are not afraid of being wrong.

Students need teachers that can help when they're having problems understanding difficult concepts. In doing so, educators may need to change how they teach the content. Since different people have unique learning styles, it's the job of the teacher to adapt to the needs of each student. Additionally, teachers should encourage students to explore alternate problem-solving strategies, even if it's not the preferred method of the educator.

FEAR OF BEING WRONG

Embarrassing situations can be traumatic, especially for young children and adolescents. These experiences can stay with people through their adult lives. Those with math anxiety may experience a fear of being wrong, especially in front of a group of peers. This fear can be paralyzing, interfering with the student's concentration and ability to focus on the problem at hand.

TIMED ASSESSMENTS

Timed assessments can help improve math fluency, but they often create unnecessary pressure for students to complete an unrealistic number of problems within a specified timeframe. Many studies have shown that timed assessments often result in increased levels of anxiety, reducing a student's overall competence and ability to problem-solve.

Debunking Math Myths

There are lots of myths about math that are related to the causes and development of math-related anxiety. Although these myths have been proven to be false, many people take them as fact. Let's go over a few of the most common myths about learning math.

MYTH: MEN ARE BETTER AT MATH THAN WOMEN

Math has a reputation for being a male-dominant subject, but this doesn't mean that men are inherently better at math than women. Many famous mathematical discoveries have been made by women. Katherine Johnson, Dame Mary Lucy Cartwright, and Marjorie Lee Brown are just a few of the many famous women mathematicians. Expecting to be good or bad at math because of your gender sets you up for stress and confusion. Math is a skill that can be learned, just like cooking or riding a bike.

MYTH: THERE IS ONLY ONE GOOD WAY TO SOLVE MATH PROBLEMS

There are many ways to get the correct answer when it comes to math. No two people have the same brain, so everyone takes a slightly different approach to problem-solving. Moreover, there isn't one way of problem-solving that's superior to another. Your way of working through a problem might differ from someone else's, and that is okay. Math can be a highly individualized process, so the best method for you should be the one that makes you feel the most comfortable and makes the most sense to you.

MYTH: MATH REQUIRES A GOOD MEMORY

For many years, mathematics was taught through memorization. However, learning in such a way hinders the development of critical thinking and conceptual understanding. These skill sets are much more valuable than basic memorization. For instance, you might be great at memorizing mathematical formulas, but if you don't understand what they mean, then you can't apply them to different scenarios in the real world. When a student is working from memory, they are limited in the strategies available to them to problem-solve. In other words, they assume there is only one correct way to do the math, which is the method they memorized. Having a variety of problem-solving options can help students figure out which method works best for them. Additionally, it provides students with a better understanding of how and why certain mathematical strategies work. While memorization can be helpful in some instances, it is not an absolute requirement for mathematicians.

MYTH: MATH IS NOT CREATIVE

Math requires imagination and intuition. Contrary to popular belief, it is a highly creative field. Mathematical creativity can help in developing new ways to think about and solve problems. Many people incorrectly assume that all things are either creative or analytical. However, this black-and-white view is limiting because the field of mathematics involves both creativity and logic.

MYTH: MATH ISN'T SUPPOSED TO BE FUN

Whoever told you that math isn't supposed to be fun is a liar. There are tons of math-based activities and games that foster friendly competition and engagement. Math is often best learned through play, and lots of mobile apps and computer games exemplify this.

Additionally, math can be an exceptionally collaborative and social experience. Studying or working through problems with a friend often makes the process a lot more fun. The excitement and satisfaction of solving a difficult problem with others is quite rewarding. Math can be fun if you look for ways to make it more collaborative and enjoyable.

MYTH: NOT EVERYONE IS CAPABLE OF LEARNING MATH

There's no such thing as a "math person." Although many people think that you're either good at math or you're not, this is simply not true. Everyone is capable of learning and applying mathematics. However, not everyone learns the same way. Since each person has a different learning style, the trick is to find the strategies and learning tools that work best for you. Some people learn best through hands-on experiences, and others find success through the use of visual aids. Others are auditory learners and learn best by hearing and listening. When people are overwhelmed or feel that math is too hard, it's often because they haven't found the learning strategy that works best for them.

MYTH: GOOD MATHEMATICIANS WORK QUICKLY AND NEVER MAKE MISTAKES

There is no prize for finishing first in math. It's not a race, and speed isn't a measure of your ability. Good mathematicians take their time to ensure their work is accurate. As you gain more experience and practice, you will naturally become faster and more confident.

Additionally, everyone makes mistakes, including good mathematicians. Mistakes are a normal part of the problem-solving process, and they're not a bad thing. The important thing is that we take the time to learn from our mistakes, understand where our misconceptions are, and move forward.

MYTH: YOU DON'T NEED MATH IN THE REAL WORLD

Our day-to-day lives are so infused with mathematical concepts that we often don't even realize when we're using math in the real world. In fact, most people tend to underestimate how much we do math in our everyday lives. It's involved in an enormous variety of daily activities such as shopping, baking, finances, and gardening, as well as in many careers, including architecture, nursing, design, and sales.

Tips and Strategies for Overcoming Math Anxiety

If your anxiety is getting in the way of your level of mathematical engagement, then there are lots of steps you can take. Check out the strategies below to start building confidence in math today.

FOCUS ON UNDERSTANDING, NOT MEMORIZATION

Don't drive yourself crazy trying to memorize every single formula or mathematical process. Instead, shift your attention to understanding concepts. Those who prioritize memorization over conceptual understanding tend to have lower achievement levels in math. Students who memorize may be able to complete some math, but they don't understand the process well enough to apply it to different situations. Memorization comes with time and practice, but it won't help alleviate math anxiety. On the other hand, conceptual understanding will give you the building blocks of knowledge you need to build up your confidence.

REPLACE NEGATIVE SELF-TALK WITH POSITIVE SELF-TALK

Start to notice how you think about yourself. Whenever you catch yourself thinking something negative, try replacing that thought with a positive affirmation. Instead of continuing the negative thought, pause to reframe the situation. For ideas on how to get started, take a look at the table below:

Instead of thinking...	Try thinking...
"I can't do this math." "I'm not a math person."	"I'm up for the challenge, and I'm training my brain in math."
"This problem is too hard."	"This problem is hard, so this might take some time and effort. I know I can do this."
"I give up."	"What strategies can help me solve this problem?"
"I made a mistake, so I'm not good at this."	"Everyone makes mistakes. Mistakes help me to grow and understand."
"I'll never be smart enough."	"I can figure this out, and I am smart enough."

PRACTICE MINDFULNESS

Practicing mindfulness and focusing on your breathing can help alleviate some of the physical symptoms of math anxiety. By taking deep breaths, you can remind your nervous system that you are not in immediate danger. Doing so will reduce your heart rate and help with any irregular breathing or shakiness. Taking the edge off of the physiological effects of anxiety will clear your mind, allowing your brain to focus its energy on problem-solving.

DO SOME MATH EVERY DAY

Think about learning math as if you were learning a foreign language. If you don't use it, you lose it. If you don't practice your math skills regularly, you'll have a harder time achieving comprehension and fluency. Set some amount of time aside each day, even if it's just for a few minutes, to practice. It might take some discipline to build a habit around this, but doing so will help increase your mathematical self-assurance.

USE ALL OF YOUR RESOURCES

Everyone has a different learning style, and there are plenty of resources out there to support all learners. When you get stuck on a math problem, think about the tools you have access to, and use them when applicable. Such resources may include flashcards, graphic organizers, study guides, interactive notebooks, and peer study groups. All of these are great tools to accommodate your individual learning style. Finding the tools and resources that work for your learning style will give you the confidence you need to succeed.

REALIZE THAT YOU AREN'T ALONE

Remind yourself that lots of other people struggle with math anxiety, including teachers, nurses, and even successful mathematicians. You aren't the only one who panics when faced with a new or challenging problem. It's probably much more common than you think. Realizing that you aren't alone in your experience can help put some distance between yourself and the emotions you feel about math. It also helps to normalize the anxiety and shift your perspective.

ASK QUESTIONS

If there's a concept you don't understand and you've tried everything you can, then it's okay to ask for help! You can always ask your teacher or professor for help. If you're not learning math in a traditional classroom, you may want to join a study group, work with a tutor, or talk to your friends. More often than not, you aren't the only one of your peers who needs clarity on a mathematical concept. Seeking understanding is a great way to increase self-confidence in math.

REMEMBER THAT THERE'S MORE THAN ONE WAY TO SOLVE A PROBLEM

Since everyone learns differently, it's best to focus on understanding a math problem with an approach that makes sense to you. If the way it's being taught is confusing to you, don't give up. Instead, work to understand the problem using a different technique. There's almost always more than one problem-solving method when it comes to math. Don't get stressed if one of them doesn't make sense to you. Instead, shift your focus to what does make sense. Chances are high that you know more than you think you do.

VISUALIZATION

Visualization is the process of creating images in your mind's eye. Picture yourself as a successful, confident mathematician. Think about how you would feel and how you would behave. What would your work area look like? How would you organize your belongings? The more you focus on something, the more likely you are to achieve it. Visualizing teaches your brain that you can achieve whatever it is that you want. Thinking about success in mathematics will lead to acting like a successful mathematician. This, in turn, leads to actual success.

FOCUS ON THE EASIEST PROBLEMS FIRST

To increase your confidence when working on a math test or assignment, try solving the easiest problems first. Doing so will remind you that you are successful in math and that you do have what it takes. This process will increase your belief in yourself, giving you the confidence you need to tackle more complex problems.

FIND A SUPPORT GROUP

A study buddy, tutor, or peer group can go a long way in decreasing math-related anxiety. Such support systems offer lots of benefits, including a safe place to ask questions, additional practice with mathematical concepts, and an understanding of other problem-solving explanations that may work better for you. Equipping yourself with a support group is one of the fastest ways to eliminate math anxiety.

REWARD YOURSELF FOR WORKING HARD

Recognize the amount of effort you're putting in to overcome your math anxiety. It's not an easy task, so you deserve acknowledgement. Surround yourself with people who will provide you with the positive reinforcement you deserve.

Remember, You Can Do This!

Conquering a fear of math can be challenging, but there are lots of strategies that can help you out. Your own beliefs about your mathematical capabilities can limit your potential. Working toward a growth mindset can have a tremendous impact on decreasing math-related anxiety and building confidence. By knowing the symptoms of math anxiety and recognizing common misconceptions about learning math, you can develop a plan to address your fear of math. Utilizing the strategies discussed can help you overcome this anxiety and build the confidence you need to succeed.

Thank You

We at Mometrix would like to extend our heartfelt thanks to you, our friend and patron, for allowing us to play a part in your journey. It is a privilege to serve people from all walks of life who are unified in their commitment to building the best future they can for themselves.

The preparation you devote to these important testing milestones may be the most valuable educational opportunity you have for making a real difference in your life. We encourage you to put your heart into it—that feeling of succeeding, overcoming, and yes, conquering will be well worth the hours you've invested.

We want to hear your story, your struggles and your successes, and if you see any opportunities for us to improve our materials so we can help others even more effectively in the future, please share that with us as well. **The team at Mometrix would be absolutely thrilled to hear from you!** So please, send us an email (support@mometrix.com) and let's stay in touch.

> **If you'd like some additional help, check out these other resources we offer for your exam:**
> **http://MometrixFlashcards.com/Iowa**

Additional Bonus Material

Due to our efforts to try to keep this book to a manageable length, we've created a link that will give you access to all of your additional bonus material:

mometrix.com/bonus948/iowal13g7